John Sam Jones was born in Barmouth on the north-west coast of Wales in 1956. After secondary school at Ysgol Ardudwy in Harlech he went on to study biology at Aberystwyth University, and then theology as a World Council of Churches Scholar in Berkeley, California. He realised he was gay as a teenager at the beginning of the 1970s and began his life-long coming out at the age of eighteen.

His collection of short stories – *Welsh Boys Too* – was an Honor Book winner in the American Library Association Stonewall Book Awards. His second collection was the acclaimed *Fishboys of Vernazza*, which was short-listed for the Wales Book of the Year. He has also published two novels *With Angels and Furies* and *Crawling Through Thorns*. He published a memoir *The Journey is Home, Notes from a Life on the Edge* in 2021 which also appeared in Welsh, translated by Sian Northey, as *Y Daith Ydi Adra, Stori Gŵr ar y Ffin*.

After working in ministry, education and public health for more than thirty years, John lives with his husband in a small German village a stone's throw from the Dutch border.

Praise for John Sam Jones's fiction

'This hugely enjoyable collection of short stories by John Sam Jones provides an insight into everything from the desire to be a parent to being coshed with a stubby fencing picket following a disappointing woodland liaison... poignant, often touching stories lead one to conclude that we are what we are but considering the deep-seated prejudice which unbelievably still exists in the 21st century, some of us are more comfortable facing the truth than others.' *The Big Issue*

'*Welsh Boys Too*, addressing the lives of gay men in contemporary Wales, was immediately recognised as a ground-breaking moment in Welsh writing in English... in this new collection of ten well-crafted stories, Jones writes as a returned native confronting the entrenched prejudice that has too often driven Welsh gay men into permanent exile... it reminds us that gay Wales is not just a minority concern.' *Planet*

'Jones writes sensitive, skillful and fat-free stories. This book is a must... and would make an excellent starting-point for anyone wishing to dip into queer fiction for the first time.' *gwales.com*

'John Sam Jones created a storm with his first collection of stories, *Welsh Boys Too*, about homosexuality in Wales. Now he has followed up his award-winning book with another sensual collection of stories... A former chair of the advisory body on gay and lesbian issues to the Assembly, Jones is not one to shy away from the questions faced by his characters... clever, poignant and perceptive.' *The Daily Post*

'Offers an alternative definition of what it means to be a man in Wales... breaks free of old clichés of masculine identity.' *New Welsh Review*

'An interracial gay couple baby-sits the two young children of a friend for a weekend; a high school boy grapples with his emergent sexuality while looking for support from the conservative adults in his life; and a mentally disturbed woman seeks vengeance against the brother who slept with her husband, in John Sam Jones's **Welsh Boys Too**. These intriguing short stories look at homosexuality through the lens of Welsh culture, subtly linking homophobia to other kinds of discrimination – racism, religious intolerance – with objectivity and sensitivity.' *Publisher's Weekly*

'**Welsh Rarebit** – John Sam Jones's charming, thoughtful collection of Welsh stories, **Welsh Boys Too**, is a joy to read. Contemporary, yet timeless, these tales of young men living in rural Wales have a pathos and dignity to them that sustains this slim, but vibrant collection. Rustic homophobia tends to be insidious rather than blatant, and Jones's subtlety of language and style highlight this, as does the wild, unsophisticated backdrop of the slopes of Cader Idris, or the seagulls circling the cliffs of the barely inhabited island of Enlli. Unsophisticated these men may be, unscathed they are not – but they are survivors, and their stories are as uplifting as they are sad. Treat yourselves.' Sebastian Beaumont in *Gay Times*

'**Welsh Boys Too** is a bold and adventurous collection of stories inspired by the lives of gay men in Wales. Funny, poignant and ultimately revealing, it introduces John Sam Jones as a new voice in the world of Welsh fiction. After spending years away from home, studying in California and as a chaplain in Liverpool, Jones returned to North Wales to be saddened by the prevailing homophobia within society and began, through writing, to explore the lives of the gay men who lived there. In a sequence of short, pointed stories, seen through the eyes of eight men, he discloses, in an often humorous manner, how they try to live their lives in a society where rejection is second nature.' *The Western Mail*

'...John Sam Jones has balanced this short anthology well; each story earns its space and does not take away from any of the other works presented. An example of this balance is the collection's ability not to shy away from sex whilst not sensationalising it either.' Adam Lewis in *Gair Rhydd*

'Cymreictod ynddo'i hun yw un o'r pethau sy'n ein gwneud ni'n fwy cul... ac mae'r iaith Gymraeg yn arf yn erbyn pobl hoyw. Dyna un rheswm pam fod Cymro Cymraeg wedi penderfynu cyhoeddi ei straeon byrion Cymreig eu naws yn uniaith Saesneg... Mae **Welsh Boys Too** gan John Sam Jones yn gasgliad o wyth stori fer sy'n trafod gwahanol agweddau o fywydau dynion hoyw yng Nghymru.' Cerys Bowen, *Golwg*

'The eight quite short stories in this thin yet evocative first-ever collection of queer fiction from Wales open the door, with fluid charm, on yet another culture's take on coming out, AIDS, homophobia and domestic togetherness. Though undeniably contemporary there is at the same time an other-worldliness to the author's world; the familiar is filtered through the gaze of a culture which is as distinct from that of America, or even England, as, for example, Italy's might be, or that of Greece. Makes for fiction that's both absorbing and entertainingly anthropological.' Richard Labonte

'Packing eight stories into a slim paperback, Jones is a paragon of economy. In the five-page 'But Names Will Never Hurt Me,' he gives us everything necessary to understand why the 17-year-old protagonist, who has already made his affectional choices, decides that 'Rent boy ... didn't sound so bad.' In nine unhurried pages, 'The Magenta Silk Thread' reveals exactly why a 77-year-old war widow is attending her best friend's son's wedding and taking the train rather than getting a lift to it. Altogether, these stories present a cross-section of a new embattled minority within an old one–Welsh gay men. Jones's examples embrace both terms of their identity. Several proudly speak Welsh, and all must come to terms with dour Welsh Calvinism as they do the public dance of appearances that being gay often requires. Jones makes them all vivid and sympathetic, not least by changing narrative perspective from story to story, from first-person subjective to third-person omniscient and even to second-person imperative.'
Ray Olson, Booklist, American Library Association.

For Jupp

Kiss and Tell

John Sam Jones

PARTHIAN

Parthian, Cardigan SA43 1ED
www.parthianbooks.com
© 2021
All Rights Reserved
ISBN 9781913640460
Editor: Gwen Davies
Cover design: Syncopated Pandemonium
Typeset by Elaine Sharples
Printed by 4edge Limited
Published with the financial support of the Welsh Books Council
British Library Cataloguing in Publication Data
A cataloguing record for this book is available from the British Library.

Contents

Tidy: an introduction

David Llewellyn

I first encountered the stories of John Sam Jones in my first few months of living in Cardiff. I'd been out and proud while studying at Dartington College, a leftfield art school in rural Devon, but moving to the city was my first real experience of a 'gay scene'.

Before then, my interaction with queer culture was limited to films and books. I read William Burroughs' *Naked Lunch* as a precocious, wide-eyed 14-year-old, and at sixteen watched Derek Jarman's *Sebastiane* in my bedroom on a black and white portable TV. Channel 4's adaptation of *Tales of the City* sent me to Armistead Maupin's charming page turners, while Vito Russo's *The Celluloid Closet* and the documentary based on it changed the way I would watch *Ben Hur* forever.

Many of the books were by American writers, the novels telling stories set on the other side of the world or in the recent past. What I was missing was a sense of myself on the page. I was a working class kid from the valleys and I fancied boys; there wasn't anyone like me in anything I read.

Over those first few months in the city I went to bars and clubs and met lots of new friends, some of whom were involved in the arts. While working on a film script that never became a film the producer gave me a copy of the recently published *Welsh Boys Too*;

the cover a sepia image of a man's bare chest and shoulder in close-up, the tip of a Roman-type sword pressed against his flesh.

Here were stories of the gay boys of Wales, the index of titles accompanied by character names like Dyfan, Rhodri and Gethin. For someone who had gone to art school pronouncing 'year', 'here', 'hear' and 'ear' exactly the same, it was refreshing, and though some of those stories were about the difficulties of coming out in the era of AIDS and Section 28 there were also gleeful tales of sex, romance and acceptance.

Re-reading them after twenty years I felt an almost Proustian rush seeing a mention of the gay travel guide *Spartacus,* which once graced the coffee tables of more affluent friends and the shelves of Waterstones' 'Lesbian & Gay' section, becoming a digital-only publication in 2017. Other stories are a reminder of how far we've come. If we were to set them in the present day, some of the characters living with their 'special friends' might now be living with husbands or long-term partners or boyfriends, without the need for euphemisms.

I first read them around the time I came out to my immediate family, which I can only describe as a beautiful anti-climax. I'd been prepared for them to cut me off, to banish me from ever darkening their doorstep again. To my pleasant surprise my parents said they already knew, and my then-teenage brother said, 'Tidy.'

It shouldn't have been a surprise, but I grew up in a place where gay men were ridiculed and despised in everyday speech, even by the occasional school teacher. When I was outed in my last year it began months of insults, culminating in one changing room fight and a later punch in the face from a complete stranger. In reading these stories from our recent past we can only hope things in Wales have changed – and continue to change – for the better.

In that sense, these stories are unavoidably of their time, but read with all this hindsight what struck me is how fresh they feel. In *Sharks on the Bedroom Floor* we're reminded of the slate industry's historic ties to slave plantations in the Caribbean, a point that resonates in the age of Black Lives Matter and the downing of statues. The theme of family recurs throughout, and the domestic scenes are beautifully observed, even when things are almost unbearable, as in *The Wedding Invitation,* its protagonist Seth experiencing the opposite of *Hiraeth*. I am fairly confident that whatever your age, you will recognise relatives, friends and maybe even lovers in these pages.

In many stories Welsh identity is as important a theme as sexuality. Characters to-and-fro between north Wales and the cities of northwest England, each hinting at something more than simply 'home', 'freedom' or 'escape'. Others return from further afield, like California's Bodega Bay, or are bound for the continent, to Etienne and the Ligurian coast.

Another motif I noticed while rereading these stories was that of myths, legends and storytelling. A gay uncle's reading of Prince Caspian turns a bedroom carpet into shark infested waters. Elsewhere there are references to the *Mabinogion,* while *Fishboys of Vernazza* adds a strange and sexy slice of magic realism to the mix.

Language and landscape run through this collection like an interwoven thread. Language – English, Cymraeg, and even Castellano – can be a means to keep secrets, or the way in which a secret is discovered, and Jones has fun throwing mono- and bilingual characters into a room, with all the tender intimacies and interpersonal conflicts that ensue.

Though many of the stories are rooted in north Wales, these are also tales of arrival and departure and the journey in between. For every small town boy there is a proud gay man striding across the world stage, but it's when describing the Welsh landscape that the writing truly soars. The descriptions of Ynys Enlli and the Llŷn Peninsula in particular make many of these stories a precursor to the more recent phenomenon of queer nature and travel writing, as embodied in books by Mike Parker, Luke Turner and Philip Hoare.

Historically much of gay life happened behind closed doors or in the shadows. It wasn't until the second half of the last century that queer pubs and clubs became a common enough sight in larger towns and cities, and meetings between gay men were, by necessity, often furtive and illicit. In making their presence felt, the characters you'll meet here are often outdoors, swimming and hiking and travelling along country lanes, or simply basking and frolicking in the sunshine.

For John Sam Jones, the fictional journeys embarked upon by his characters have often been a reflection of his own peripatetic life. In the 1980s he lived in California, and more recently, in Brexit's aftermath, he left Wales for Germany with his German husband. It's therefore appropriate and timely that this collection of his short stories accompanies an autobiography, and that its title is *The Journey is Home*.

David Llewellyn is a novelist and script writer based in Cardiff. His most recent novel, *A Simple Scale* (Seren) was shortlisted for the Polari Prize.

WELSH BOYS TOO

The Birds Don't Sing...

Vorsicht! The word was written in bold red capitals that drew my eye; in smaller black lettering the warning of extremely dangerous high voltage, *Hochspannung... Lebensgefahr!,* was almost unreadable after fifty years of weather. The concrete post bearing this token of concern for human life was streaked with rust from the bolts that fastened the sign to it and the barbed wire it supported. I noticed the stains, the colour of iodine and dry blood, reaching down into the bouquet of carnations laid at the post's base by some earlier tourist to the site and tried to order the chaos of thoughts stumbling into each other. After staring at the intense whiteness of the carnations for a long time I decided that whoever had laid them couldn't possibly be called a tourist.

The same thought process led me to wonder what label I could give myself; yesterday, wandering through the old market place and nosing around the cathedral with my thrusting zoom lens I'd certainly been one. And a few days before, scrambling along the Orla Perc mountain ridge, the Eagle's Path, with maps and a compass, the breathtaking snow-capped peaks inviting potentially fatal lapses in concentration, I'd been a hiker or a walker. But here, in this place, without the identity offered by such labels, I didn't know who I was.

We'd chosen Zakopane for two reasons: no cheap charter flight, and a friend's recommendation. Some of the boys from the Gay Outdoor Club had been there and spent a '...spectacular... wonderful... brill' week walking in the Tatra Mountains. Gwyn had said that it was like having a Snowdonia the size of Wales to explore, but then, Gwyn was such a size-queen anyway and always professed to things being bigger than they were. And after that last trip to Gran Canaria, when there just hadn't been enough sick bags to go round all the lager louts on the midnight flight home, I'd vowed never to fly charter again, so a holiday package by coach seemed like a good idea.

Griff, who always read the guide books for weeks before we ever booked anything and memorised town plans, major street names and sights worth seeing, knew from the *Rough*, the *Blue* and the *Let's Go* that Zakopane had a past. Poland's well-heeled metropolitan consumptives had secured the town's reputation as a fashionable health resort in the 1870s. These were followed by artists and intellectuals from Kraków, their bohemian colony thriving long into the dying days of the Austro-Hungarian Empire. Then came the skiers, followed by the walkers and climbers. It was the arty connection that had finally sold it to Griff, who'd come to think of himself as one of a new breed of intellectuals since he'd won the chair at an important regional eisteddfod. And I suppose I knew, too, that he'd memorised the names of the bars, saunas and cruising areas mentioned in *Spartacus* and that Griff wanted to add a Pole or ten to the list of foreign nationals he'd knelt before.

For as long as the weather had remained warm and sunny, Zakopane and its surroundings hadn't disappointed us; we'd come to walk in the mountains and we'd done six hikes in as many near perfect days. We could tick off the Rysy, the Copper and the Sunburnt Peaks, the Upper and Lower Frogs, the Ox

Back and The High One; names, unpronounceable in Polish, that conjured up the myths and legends of the highlanders who'd once lived on their slopes. On the shore of Czarny Staw, the Black Lake, resting after a hard climb, I'd taken Griff roughly, almost violently, on a smooth, sun-warmed slab of granite. Swimming, afterwards, and bathing one another in the ice-cold water, our cocks shrank to a size that even Gwyn, for all his exaggerating, could only have mocked. On another afternoon, in a high Alpine meadow, deep in the folds of a tumbling sheet of yellow mountain leopard's bane, Griff held me to the ground and pushed deeply into me; in the peace that came after sex we lay in one another's arms and watched a golden eagle circle on a thermal. They'd been good days. In the evenings we'd eaten at the Watra or the Jerus, drank coffee in street cafés and only much later gone to Janina's bar to sip iced vodka and flirt with the two waiters, Leszek and Jakub. Neither had played hard to get.

The mist and rain had begun to fall into the valleys of the Tatras on the eighth day, and Zakopane winced under the burden of a swirling damp that pressed its rooftops low. I'd read for most of the day while Griff cruised the park and cottaged in the public toilet by the bus station. In the late afternoon we'd met for coffee and sticky pastries in the hotel lounge. Griff's bit of rough in the bushes had left him feeling chilled, however, and he soon left to loll in a hot bath. I stayed in the lounge to eat just one more sticky pastry and wonder what we might do for the remaining days if the weather didn't improve. Licking my fingers clean of the syrup from the pastry my eye was caught by the questioning gaze of a striking older woman whom I took, from the elegance of her dress, to be German. As she walked towards me, I realised that all the tables in the lounge were occupied by groups of hotel guests, their plans frustrated by the weather, sharing anecdotes:

The regal architecture of Kraków... The excitement and sheer terror of the raft ride through the Dunajec Gorge... The rickety local buses... When she asked if she might join me at my table her American accent, though surprising my earlier assumption, made me relax.

Over a small pot of coffee that the waiter had brought us, I discovered that Marlene taught German literature at the University of California in Berkeley, that her husband never came on any of her trips to Europe, and that she was in Poland to visit her sister. I felt easy with her. She was interesting, liked to talk and didn't ask too many questions. She was German, but had left for America in 1947; she had three grown up sons, all lawyers like their father, and her mother, at ninety-three, still lived in a resplendent Victorian in San Francisco's Pacific Heights. She ordered aperitifs for us both and continued her story.

They'd had a difficult war, according to family legend, but since she'd been born in 1932, her memories were mostly those of a happy schoolgirl. She recalled that her mother's American citizenship had created some problems and that they'd had to go to the police station almost every day to register. She remembered, too, that her father, a theology professor, had brushed with the Gestapo because of his professional relationship with Dietrich Bonhoeffer. Then there had been the business with her little sister, Hannelore. Some of the California sunshine went out of her face when she explained that they took all children with Down's Syndrome to a state hospital, though they had managed to hide her right up until 1943.

I had begun to feel uncomfortable as the bleakness of the memories hardened Marlene's face. I sensed that her immediate thoughts, worlds away from the words she'd spoken, might bring us to the edge of an intimacy that would be improper after so little time. I told her that we, Griff and I, were in Zakopane to walk, and as I said it, I realised that she'd become embarrassed by my unease.

Marlene eventually breached the silence that had cut between us like a mountain gorge. She asked whether Griff was a special friend. I knew that she knew. When she began to talk about her son Matt and his lover Kip, I realised that what Griff called 'gay man's mother's intuition' had seen through me. Eased by the new understanding between us she had become animated once again. She explained how she'd tried to persuade Matt and Kip to make the trip to Europe with her, but Kip had balked at the idea, as had Matt who didn't consider those tens of thousands with pink triangles as his brothers. I heard myself say that I'd go with her. For hours afterwards I tried to convince myself that I was only going because of the rain.

We moved away from the blood stained concrete post with its bouquet of carnations. We walked on in the silence that had closed over us as we'd stood before the huge mound of women's hair; a silence that numbed as we looked into the eyes of a child with Down's, sitting on the infamous doctor's knee, smiling from a photograph. It was an external silence only; inside me was a screaming bedlam. At the railway tracks, overgrown with wild grasses and purple-headed thistles, we sat on one of the iron rails. Overwhelmed by the malignity of the scene, I recalled the frightened eyes and the hate-scarred faces of the people in my own village. I'd been interviewed for a television programme about the age of consent for gay men. I heard again their insults and their jibes. I smelled the dog shit that someone had put through our letterbox and the paint of the words *Queers Out* daubed on our garage doors. As my thoughts became too painful I turned away.

'The birds sing beautifully here,' I offered after a while. Marlene, her face haunted, looked into my eyes.

'No,' she corrected, 'they say Kaddish and recite Psalms, but they do not sing. The birds don't sing in Auschwitz.'

Sharks on the Bedroom Floor

Rhodri

The first you knew of the pirates' ambush was the blow to your head. In the disorientation that followed, and to the sound of excited screeches and a gutsy 'Com'on mi hearties' from the children, you worried whether Justin had put his pyjama bottoms back on after you'd made love. Your unease became palpable on realising that they might discover your own morning stand bulging in your boxer shorts if they got under the duvet. Sensational headlines from tabloid newspapers jarred your mind. And where had the knotted condom ended up after you'd fallen asleep in Justin's embrace?

Penri, his left eye covered by a make-shift eye patch, jarred his knee unknowingly against your erection and pushed onto your aching bladder as he raised the pillow and struck again, hitting you hard across your bare chest. Tirion, by far the more placid of the two but looking fierce brandishing a loofah, bounced into the air before launching herself with a near primal scream across Justin, who caught her before she fell from the deck of the imaginary ship into the sea of sharks on the bedroom floor. You lifted your nephew an arm's length into the blue sky above the besieged schooner, dropped him gently into Justin's arms beside his sister, and avoiding the sharks that snapped at bare feet and indecent exposure, escaped to the bathroom.

Justin

You had always seemed more at ease with Tirion and Penri, probably because you never felt the need to second-guess the multiplicity of motives, ignoble or otherwise, behind your actions like Rhodri did. You pacified the marauding pirates by agreeing to read more of *Prince Caspian* and the children's adventures (two of whom just happened to be called Tirion and Penri) in Narnia. They liked it when their uncle Justin read to them in English. Sometimes they stopped you to ask the meanings of words and you would realise again that they spoke only Welsh with their parents in a home where the use of English was not encouraged. You remembered the heated argument with Gwydion, their father, who'd maintained that because English was so dominant anyway, discouraging its use in their home wouldn't disadvantage the children. You, whom Rhodri considered as English as Colman's Mustard but retaining ancestral vestiges of taste for Caribbean spices that were much less bland, had suggested that Gwydion's politics might have skewed his acute intelligence. Loving you for the stability brought to Rhodri's life, Gwydion had reacted with uncharacteristic tolerance, thinking deeply about what you'd said. But then he hadn't changed his mind. After that family storm, your reading to the children, whenever they came to stay, had become a mission. As well as all of Lewis' Narnia tales you read them Roald Dahl and even poems by Larkin and Robert Graves; how many times had they shouted 'Again uncle Justin... Again' after the final 'I was coming to that' in *Welsh Incident*?

Rhodri

When you came back into the bedroom you found the stricken schooner re-imagined; Justin the Dwarf was propped up against the pillows, a child nuzzling under each arm, and they were rowing in a boat, eastward around the tip of a magical island. Tirion brought her index finger up to her mouth sharply with a 'Shhh!' and explained to you in Welsh, her excitement overflowing, that they'd reached a good bit. Justin, with a wink and a smile, carried on reading in a suitably dwarfish voice: 'Beards and bedsteads! So there really is a castle, after all?' You pulled on your jeans and wondered how different the scene might be if the children weren't just borrowed; if they were yours and Justin's how quickly would they tire of being read to and become the *diawliaid bach*, the little devils their mother claimed them to be?

Before you'd finished laying the table for breakfast, you heard Penri's crying, quickly followed by an avalanche on the back stairs. When he burst into the kitchen you took in the disaster that had befallen the little chap: so bound had he been by the magic of Narnia, he'd peed himself. Taking him up into your arms, you told him that it didn't matter and that life was hard when you were five and a half. Consoling Penri wasn't made any easier once Tirion arrived in the kitchen. Grumpy and disconsolate because Justin the Dwarf had stopped reading and begun to strip the bed of the wet sheet and mattress cover, she teased and baited her little brother and said that she'd be sure to tell *Mam* about him wetting uncle Rhodri and uncle Justin's bed.

Tirion
Carelessly pushing a spoon around your cereal bowl trying to fish out the last pearls of soggy puffed wheat you explained why Quaker's were nicer than Tesco's own brand.

'Sugar Puffs are just too sweet and not at all healthy,' you'd just announced with authority, prompting Justin to ask if you'd done a degree in breakfast cereals. Laughing at his suggestion, you

11

added, rather too seriously for a nine-year-old, that you'd like to study history at university because you liked learning about the Celts and slates and you liked reading *Y Mabinogion*. And when you grew up you were going to teach at a university just like your mother. But you didn't know what physics was yet, except that it was science and that your mother was the only one of her kind.

'What do you know about slates, then?' Rhodri asked, laughing. You talked about your class project on the Penrhyn Quarry at Bethesda where some people your mother called *ein cyndeidiau* had slaved.

'The biggest slates are over 700 millimetres long – they're called 'queens', you explained, stretching out your arms. You described with precision how the great slabs of slate were docked, split and dressed.

'I can't remember exactly how they came out of the mountain – they were exploded.'

Justin asked if you'd learnt about John Pennant and his son Richard, the men who'd first opened up the quarry in the 1780s? Shaking your head you looked blank while Penri shrieked with delight as one of the nameless barn cats caught one of the starlings that had settled on the lawn to feed.

Justin

After the committal of the dead starling in a coffin that had been shaped from an empty Quaker Puffed Wheat carton, you drove off with Tirion to the nursery to look for Spiked Speedwells, Anchusas, Blue African Lilies, and anything else blue for the new border. Your vision for the six and a half acres of hill-side that rolled gently down to the river Clwyd included a succession of small gardens each planted up in one colour and linked by arbours of clematis and honeysuckle and climbing roses; *Compassion* was your favourite, with its pinky-apricot flowers and heady scent. Rhodri's grand plan for Hafod Ilan Hall, which you bought after your office syndicate scooped nearly eleven million on the lottery, is to open the place up as a stress management cum retreat centre with workshops on reflexology and aromatherapy, relaxation and massage as well as courses on time management. There would be lots of beautiful, quiet places for your hefty-fee-paying executive guests to unwind from the self-importance of their corporate worlds.

Tirion

Driving together to the nursery, you weren't sure what you wanted to ask uncle Justin, whom you knew very little about. You knew that uncle Rhodri was your daddy's brother and that he'd been your mammy's best friend when they were students in Aberystwyth. Perhaps uncle Justin had been in Aberystwyth too? It did seem to you as though he'd always been around, at least for as long as you could remember. There were pictures of him in the albums from the time when Penri had been born or perhaps a few pages before... But he wasn't in Mammy and Daddy's wedding pictures, so perhaps he hadn't been in Aberystwyth! That he didn't speak Welsh hadn't been enough of a difference to arouse curiosity; after all, Mrs Gittins, the lady who cleaned the house didn't speak Welsh and neither did your best friend's father. For that matter, lots of the people your mother worked with at the university, who sometimes came to the house, couldn't speak Welsh. You couldn't remember when the shiny blackness of his skin had become tangible as the difference that had kindled your fascination in him. Perhaps it had been after seeing something on the television about Tutsis and Hutus in Rwanda; you remembered how you'd liked the sound of those names, voicing them over and over and asking your mother if uncle Justin was from there. She'd laughed and said that he was

13

from Liverpool, where you'd been once, to the theatre to see *Joseph*.

Rhodri

Watching his sister and uncle Justin driving away after the starling's funeral, Penri threw a tantrum, jealous that Tirion was getting the greater share of Justin's attention. Quietly regretting that you hadn't taken Tirion for the morning, you tried reading to him from *Prince Caspian*, but still he cried. You sang one of the nonsense action songs you'd learnt at the *Urdd* summer camp at Llangrannog more than twenty years before (with thigh slapping, hand shaking and head tapping), but that made Penri screech even louder. You tried to lift him, to offer him reassurance, but Penri hammered his clenched fists against your chest. You thought about giving him a good slap across the back of his legs to give him something to cry about; that had been your own mother's way and it had always seemed to have the desired effect. But you knew well enough that Gwydion and Eleri had never hit their children; their discipline was based on 'time-out' and loss of privileges. As sternly as you could, you sent Penri into the back living room and told him to stay there until he was ready to be sociable. To your great surprise the tactic worked; in less than ten minutes Penri came into the kitchen, his face bright and smiling (but still a bit red around the eyes) asking, 'Can we let the chickens out and collect the eggs from the hen house?'

Tirion

No... Uncle Justin hadn't been in Aberystwyth... He knew uncle Rhodri from work... Yes, they'd both worked in the same office at the hospital for a while until he'd moved to the personnel department... That's right, before they'd stopped working and gone to live in Hafod Ilan.

14

'And have I got a mammy? Yes, she still lives in Liverpool with my father.'

You laughed because he'd given you the wrong answer.

'No, I mean like my daddy's got my mammy.'

Perhaps sensing that you were working something out or to give himself a moment to think, Justin asked you if you knew the name for the relationship between your mother and father. Thoughtfully, you spoke some terms in Welsh and after a few moments' word searching in your English vocabulary you said, 'They're married and they're husband and wife.' You caught on to his word game.

'Have you got a wife, then?' you asked.

'You know I haven't got a wife, Tirion... I've got uncle Rhodri.'

You went quiet for some minutes and then asked perplexedly what their relationship was called, 'You can't both be husbands, can you?'

Justin

You smiled at her logical conclusion and thought about the terms you and Rhodri used to describe your life together; friends, partners, lovers even spouses, but you heard yourself saying, 'It's called living together, we're special friends.' The answer seemed to satisfy her because she looked out of the window for a long while before she asked you about Richard Pennant and the slate quarry.

'Do you know where Jamaica is?'

She laughed, thinking you were being silly, and asked, 'What has an island somewhere far away got to do with Richard Pennant and my school project?' You pulled into the nursery so you said you'd tell her the story later.

15

Penri

After marking the date carefully on each of the newly laid eggs with a date stamp (that uncle Rhodri had shown you how to roll gently over the shells so as not to break them), together you put eighteen into three egg boxes, laying four under the pottery hen that nested on the work-top next to the kettle. You took the three boxes to the village shop where Mrs Jones gave you both a welcome. 'We always have customers for Hafod Ilan eggs,' she smiled a yellow, bad toothed smile and offered you a *Kit-Kat*. 'What else are you going to do to be a good boy for your uncle?'

'We're going to plant potatoes,' you told her, 'but we have to go up to the riding school first to get some manure.'

She laughed, showing the black teeth at the back of her gnarled mouth, and said, 'And they're sure to be good potatoes if you grow them in horse muck.'

Holding the bag open for your uncle Rhodri to fork in the manure, you asked if all mammies and daddies picked one another the way you'd seen them do on the television. Rhodri, completely at a loss to know what you were talking about, asked you what you'd seen. You described the way a girl had asked three boys some questions and then picked the one she wanted to marry. Rhodri explained that going on television shows like that was just a bit of fun and that the boys and girls weren't really looking for someone to marry... But you lost all interest in your uncle Rhodri's explanations when one of your wellingtons got caught in a sludgy part of the manure heap; it sank even deeper as you tried to wriggle it free and before Rhodri had a chance to grab you, you'd fallen face down into the steaming horse shit. Rhodri laughed, until he realised that you, spitting straw and dirt from your mouth, were beside yourself; at first you bawled from the fright and shock of it all and then you whimpered until long after getting back to Hafod Ilan.

Tirion

You didn't understand how people could be bought and sold or how one person could actually own another one. Justin's account was full of facts – like school, but he brought the story to life, just like he had when he'd read from *Prince Caspian* to you that morning. He described how the ships from Liverpool carried to West Africa fine materials manufactured by the cloth and wool merchants in Yorkshire and Lancashire, china from the Potteries and guns made in Birmingham.

'The white people traded these goods for slaves. Black people, just like me, my great great great great grandparents and uncles and aunties and cousins. They were hoarded into the holds of Liverpool ships with hardly enough food and water, chained with leg irons, and taken to Jamaica.'

Shocked by what he was saying you'd asked, almost disbelieving him, 'Why would they want to take your family there?'

'To trade them for sugar from the big plantations,' he'd said. 'One of the biggest and richest was the Clarendon. Thomas Pennant was the owner, the same man who owned the Penrhyn Quarry. My family slaved for five generations to make him, and those that came after him, rich beyond imagination from the sugar and with part of his fortune he'd developed the slate quarries around Bethesda.' Your interest in slates was sullied by what you'd heard and your liking for history was affronted by what your teacher had left untold, but carrying the plants in from the back of the Land Rover you couldn't stop thinking how much more exciting your uncle Justin had become.

Rhodri

Penri had set the table for lunch and the knives and forks were mislaid; Tirion took it upon herself to re-set them and he started to cry again leaving you wondering how Eleri and Gwydion coped with such a snivelling child (and thinking, too, that a good slap across the back of his legs would indeed do him some good). Justin calmed him in minutes by making an aeroplane from the credit card bill that had arrived earlier and been propped against the pepper mill. Penri threw the paper dart around the kitchen a few times until it came to a soggy end, crash-landing in the washing-up bowl. Your glare suggested something like 'that was really effing stupid' to Justin, who gingerly unfolded the sodden bill and set it on the shelf above the ancient anthracite range to dry. Penri's attention turned to the jar of Branston Pickle, his favourite, and they ate bread, cheese and pickles in a relative calm.

Tirion

Despite a sheet of nimbus unfolding and spreading itself out over the sea beyond Rhyl, you and Rhodri took a spade and a fork from one of the outhouses Justin had decided could serve as a temporary garden shed and Rhodri set about digging the furrows for the Maris Pipers. Struggling with the fork (that was at least as tall as you were), you followed on behind him slopping sometimes over generous amounts of horse muck into the furrows. It was a smelly job and you soon wished you'd gone with Penri and uncle Justin to plant the African Lilies and Speedwells which, you were sure because they had such lovely flowers, weren't grown in stinking horse manure. Rhodri, sensing your disaffection with potato planting, asked you about the poems and songs you were learning for the *Urdd eisteddfod* and about multiplication tables. Though irked by his questions, you recited one of the poems but then refused to say your tables because you always got stuck after the sevens... And all the time you were thinking about Jamaica and slaves and how it was that your uncle Justin could still be friends with uncle Rhodri after what Thomas

Pennant had done to black people from Africa. Then the rain came in heavily off the sea and you were saved from forking manure with your boring uncle Rhodri.

Rhodri
Penri had flour in his hair and on the floor and sticky dough up around his elbows, on cupboard doorknobs and all over the chair on which he stood. Soaked through by the cloudburst, you warmed yourself in front of the range and wondered where Justin had left his common sense; making scones for tea was hardly a practical way to occupy the kids for an hour. Tirion, who'd changed quickly into dry clothes so that she could join in the fun, rolled out pieces of the soggy mix for Penri and Justin to stab with the shaped cutters; she proved as menacing with the rolling pin as she'd been with the loofah and Justin bore floury weals on his arms and cheeks where she'd struck him in her play. You felt the comforting heat of the oven penetrate the dampness of your jeans and shirt, and through the warming of your body you sensed the awakening of sexual arousal. And the collision of two thoughts: the primitive and savage sexuality of Justin's flour streaked features excited you as much as the latent racism from which the fantasy arose appalled and offended you.

Drying yourself off after a hot shower you heard the phone ring. Justin called from the kitchen for you to get it on the bedroom phone as he was still covered in flour. Eleri sounded a bit down; the paper she'd delivered at the conference in Gregynog had gone well enough, but she'd been disappointed by the other contributors and decided to leave that evening so she could spend Sunday with the children. With Gwydion still in the States, Rhodri suggested she might have supper with them and stay over until the morning, otherwise it would be late by the time she and the kids got back to Anglesey and an empty house. They could crack open a few bottles of wine and put the world right until the early hours like they'd done so many times in Aber. She said she'd see.

Justin

The scones weren't too hard. You ate them with the bramble jelly you'd made at the end of the last summer. The blackberries had been picked with the children along the overgrown hedgerows through which the lane up to Hafod Ilan rambled. Rhodri suggested that perhaps, if there was a next time (for in the good half hour it had taken to clean up the mess you'd come to rue your folly), they might add a bit more lard and a bit less milk. Tirion and Penri, their mouths full of bramble jelly and scone, were oblivious to their uncle Rhodri's jibe. Cut by the sharpness of Rhodri's intonation and frustrated by his jealousy of the relationship you had with the children, you felt your anger rise and, with a stabbing stare at Rhodri, left them to their tea.

Much as you'd expected, you found the spade and garden fork that Rhodri and Tirion had used, still covered with mud and manure, dropped carelessly on the floor of the outhouse. You set about cleaning them, having long become resigned to finishing jobs which Rhodri left unfinished. You'd recognised the spoilt child in Rhodri in the first days of your coming together, and disliked the brat... But those days had passed quickly into weeks of frantic sexual pleasure when little else about the character and personality of a new lover seemed to matter, and for as long as you'd made Rhodri the myopic focus of your attentions, Rhodri, in return, had loved you in a way you'd never known. Almost imperceptibly, those indulgent weeks of heightened lusty passion had given way to the mundane reality of getting on with your everyday lives. You'd become more aware of Rhodri's spoilt child as an unwelcome intruder in the relationship, but you also began to recognise the shift from being in love with Rhodri to loving him, and in accepting his faults you found ways to cope. You finished tidying the outhouse and decided, since the rain had stopped, to walk off your unquelled anger along the riverbank.

Rhodri and Eleri were drinking red wine and preparing supper in the kitchen when you returned to the house just before six. From the almost empty bottle of Cahors and the glint in her eye you didn't have to be a detective to deduce that she'd abandoned any idea of driving on to Anglesey. Putting your jacket on the peg you saw that the children were quiet in the back living room, colouring-in with the new set of crayons and colouring books Eleri had bought them (out of guilt for being away a third weekend on the run). She'd been slow to warm to you when you'd first met, but now she kissed you affectionately and said, 'Penri's too embarrassed to say sorry for his little accident that morning.' You shrugged and smiled and said it was nothing. Your relationship had never been easy; unsurprising, since she and Rhodri had been engaged. At first you'd thought it was because she had a problem with blacks, but about a year after you and Rhodri got together the whole bizarre saga in Aberystwyth had been dredged up at a boozy family do. How Rhodri broke off their engagement when he finally came out to himself and she had married Gwydion within a year. After that little closet had been sprung open and its secrets aired, you found yourself feeling a little more sympathy for her rancour. But from then on you'd been left with the feeling that you'd won her prize and that you owed her something. Knowing all this hadn't really helped you to be at ease with her.

Rhodri

Penri liked bacon but didn't like liver or olives. Tirion didn't like olives either... Or mushrooms... Or bacon. You swapped bits of the casserole around the children's plates and quietly cursed Eleri for not saying something sooner because they could have had grilled chicken breasts instead. Justin asked her about the conference. She said it was awful and was about to elaborate when Penri asked her if she and his daddy had met on the television.

'What do you mean?' she asked, puzzled. Penri described the girl asking three boys some questions and cutting him off she asked, with an edge of disbelief, why they'd let the children watch such rubbish.

'Eat your supper and don't to be so silly,' she snapped at her son, turning again to her ongoing complaint about the conference speakers. In the lull in her soliloquy Tirion offered with great seriousness, 'I'd like to find a husband on telly when I'm older.' You laughed, but seeing Eleri scowl you offered, 'You're too gorgeous to have to look far for boyfriends.' Penri, pulling a face at his sister, said, 'You're not gorgeous – and anyway, I don't want to go on the television because I'm going to live with my best friend, Aled, just like uncle Justin and uncle Rhodri.' Both you and Justin wanted to acknowledge Penri, but Eleri gulped her wine, splurting, 'The liver is very tender!' And then Tirion asked her mother why her teacher hadn't told her class that black slaves in Jamaica had made Thomas Pennant rich and made Welsh children orphans because their daddies were killed digging for slates.

Justin and the children started to get caught up in yet another play scene from the unwritten Narnia chronicle, *Prince Penri and the Sea of Sharks*. Eleri, despite herself, was impressed with the

22

way Justin handled the children – and with his imagination! – but drew the game to a close as the sound levels rose. Everyone agreed to do a turn in a little *noson lawen*. Penri, with a bit of prompting from his mother, recited a poem in Welsh about a grandfather clock while Tirion sang about two rabbits being chased across a field. You and Eleri sang the duet that had won you both first prize in the inter-college *eisteddfod* too many years ago to remember, and as it was a Welsh Evening, Justin read *Welsh Incident* twice because the children shouted 'Again uncle Justin' after the final 'I was coming to that.'

Eleri

After the children had been settled for the night and the supper dishes stacked in the dishwasher, you drank more wine and talked in the back living room. You, though, quickly gave in to your tiredness. You slept fitfully, dreaming vivid dreams... Penri was asking three boys questions, and then he walked down the aisle with Rhodri in a wedding dress while the Harlech Silver Band played *Marchog Iesu* and the Mayor of Cricieth twisted his fingers in his chain of office. Tirion cut sugar cane on the steep terraced quarries above Bethesda, and beyond Cricieth's sea caves there was another Welsh incident: Justin the Dwarf rowed you in a boat and the sea of sharks on the bedroom floor snapped at your bare feet.

The Wonder at Seal Cave

Gethin stacked the returned books and wondered why Mr Bateman always seemed to do his marking in the middle study bay; why not the staff room, the small 'prep' room at the back of the biology lab, or even one of the other bays? Quite often, when he was putting books back in the geography section, nearest the study area, they'd smile at one another. Sometimes, if there was no one else in the library, they'd talk – but only if Mr Bateman initiated the conversation. Gethin liked these talks; he liked it that Mr Bateman seemed interested in what he was reading and what films he'd seen, or what he thought about mad cows, adulterous royals, and the war in Chechnya. Sometimes they even talked about football. When Gethin turned up for his library duty he found himself hoping that he and Mr Bateman would be alone, that there would be plenty of geography books to shelve, and that they might talk.

Mr Bateman was his favourite teacher; he was most people's favourite really. He got angry sometimes and shouted a bit, but he was never sarcastic, which seemed to be the weapon most of the male staff used to intimidate their classes into some kind of order and control. And he always made biology interesting, even if there were lots of facts that had to be memorised. He was the kind of teacher most students wanted to do well for, to please. The exam results pleased everyone; there were more A grades in biology from Ysgol yr Aber than from any other school in Wales and the school's record of success in biology was always used by the Welsh Office to challenge the cynicism of those opposed to Welsh language science education.

Mr Bateman had learned to speak Welsh; perhaps this was what Gethin liked best about him. Very few of the English people who'd settled in the area had bothered to learn the language, but he had, and Gethin was hard put to detect an ill-formed mutation or a confused gender; Mr Bateman spoke better Welsh than many native speakers and Gethin admired him for the respect he'd shown to the language and culture of his adopted home. And there was football too; Gethin thought highly of him for that! Mr Bateman had grown up in Manchester and everyone at school knew how fanatically he still supported his home team – United, not City. Gethin supported Liverpool and went to some home games with Mel Tudor, Mel-siop-baco as everyone knew him, who had a season ticket at Anfield.

Gethin carried the Welsh novels back to their shelf wondering if he dared start a conversation with Mr Bateman. He needed to talk to somebody. The school summer holidays had been such a mixed time; although he'd been confident enough of good grades, waiting for the GCSE results had found him lurching between the certainty of staying on at school to do his A-levels and the uneasy emptiness of 'What if?'. It was then that *the other thing* bothered him; it had been there for ages, of course, but 'Doing well in your exams,' and 'Going to university like your brother and sister,' had been a sufficient enough screen to hide behind. The kiss on *Brookside*, outing bishops and the debate about the age of consent had made the screen wobble a bit, but he really hadn't allowed himself to think very much that he might be, or what that might mean, until those moments of uneasy emptiness had folded over him. And now he knew that he was and he needed to talk about it.

He'd tried to talk to his sister. Gethin had stayed with Eilir in Liverpool at the beginning of July; he'd tried talking to her after seeing the film, but she'd seemed so taken up with her patients, her new boyfriend and the hassles she and her flat-mates were having with their landlord about the fungus growing on the kitchen wall. It was because she'd been so preoccupied that Gethin had spent his time in the city alone and had the chance to go to the cinema on a rainy afternoon. He'd read a review of *Beautiful Thing* in *The Guide* that came with Saturday's *Guardian*, and when he saw that it was showing at the ABC on Lime Street he'd loitered on the opposite pavement for almost an hour trying to muster up the courage to go in. It was the rain that eventually sent him through the glass doors into the garishly lit foyer of the cinema to face the spotty, many ear-ringed boy in the ticket booth who dispensed the ticket with a wry smile. Gethin had panicked, interpreting the boy's smile, as 'I know you're queer... all the boys who come to see this film on their own are!' Only after taking his seat in the darkened auditorium did his panic subside.

It was a love story; Jamie and Ste, two boys his own age, falling in love with one another. There were no steamy love scenes and but for a fleeting glance at Ste's naked bottom there was no nudity, so Gethin got few clues as to what two boys might actually do together. When Jamie and Ste ran through the trees chasing one another and finally embracing and kissing, Gethin had become aroused; he'd wanted to be Jamie in the film – to be held and kissed by Ste.... He'd wanted his own mother to be as accepting as Jamie's and he'd wanted a friend like Leah to talk to.

Outside the cinema it had stopped raining so Gethin decided to walk back to Eilir's flat near Princes Park. Wandering along Princes Avenue, he came to understand that something had changed in his life and nothing would be the same again. Behind the screen that he'd erected to keep himself from thinking about *the other thing* he'd felt closed in silence – a silence which had left him anxious and uncertain, even fearful. But the screen had been pulled away by Jamie and Ste and their story had begun to give that unspeakable part of Gethin's life a shape. For the first time Gethin really understood what his father had so often preached to his congregation – 'That stories give shape to lives and that without stories we cannot understand ourselves.' Of course, the Reverend Llŷr Jones had a certain anthology of stories in mind for giving shape to lives and Gethin knew that his father wouldn't include Jamie and Ste's story alongside those of Jacob, Jeremiah and Jesus. Llŷr Jones wouldn't see the two boys' story as a 'beautiful thing'.

Gethin recalled that Sunday during the age of consent debate. His father, in a fiery sermon, had exhorted the congregation at Tabernacl (Methodistiaid Calfinaidd – 1881) to write to the local MP urging him to vote against lowering the age to sixteen. Gethin remembered the discussion over the roast beef after chapel, his father – with all the authority of an M.Th. and a dog-collar behind his words, saying that homosexuals were sinful and his mother – in her calm 'I'm the doctor, you can trust me' manner, saying that they were disturbed and needed psychiatric treatment.

Crossing Princes Park, Gethin sat by a reservoir of the city's debris that had once been a lake. He watched a used condom navigate its course on a stiffening breeze through the squalid waters between the half-submerged skeletons of an old bike and a supermarket trolley until it came to lie, stranded on the shore of an abandoned pram. He thought about his father and mother; how he loved them – but how he now didn't think he knew them at all. If he told them about the film – about Jamie and Ste and about what he now knew to be true of himself, would his father's love be acted out in some kind of exorcism and would his mother want the best medical care with visits to some psychologist? Gethin wondered if their love and trust in him were deep enough to challenge thirty years of belief in Calvinistic Biblical scholarship and 1960s medical science? A plastic baby's arm reached from the crib of slime in which it lay, grasping an empty sky; Gethin wondered if his reaching out would be as futile. Back at the flat, Eilir wanted to talk about her first AIDS patient – and about the fungus on the kitchen wall.

Mr Bateman looked up from his marking and smiled at Gethin; he smiled back and mouthed a silent greeting which Mr Bateman returned. Gethin put the dozen or so geography books back on their shelf and turned to talk to his teacher, but his head was already back in his books. With no reason to linger by the study area and insufficient courage to go up to Mr Bateman and ask if they could talk, he fetched the remaining pile of returns and went to the science section at the other end of the library.

For some weeks after his stay in Liverpool, Gethin had tried to prop up the screen which Jamie and Ste's story had so successfully toppled. The hikes and bike rides he and his friends had arranged made hiding from the dawning truths of his life easier, but he couldn't escape the knowledge that in all games of hide-and-seek, that which was hidden was always found. Then there had been the tense days leading up to the exam results, and those few exhilarating hours which high achievement and congratulation had brought. His course of A-level study was set, and before the trough of anti-climax swallowed him he got caught up in all the preparations for Enlli; ever since he could remember, the whole family had spent the week of August bank holiday on the remote island. Everyone had thought that this year would be different – that Seifion, Gethin's brother, wouldn't be able to come home from America; but then Seifion had phoned to say that his newspaper needed him back in London for the first week in September, so he'd be with them after all. For a whole week, Gethin packed all the provisions they'd need on the island into boxes that were then wrapped in black bin bags to keep everything dry during the trip in the open boat across the sound. At least this year they didn't have to take all their drinking water too!

Their week on Enlli was, for different reasons, special to each member of the family. His mother liked the peace and unhurried simplicity of life without electricity and phones, cars and supermarket queues – and patients! She'd sometimes come in from a walk and say things like 'Mae bywyd ar yr ynys 'ma yn gneud i rywun gwestiynnu daliadau'r oes gyfoes – Life here makes you question so much of what we think is important on the mainland,' to anyone who happened to be in ear-shot, but such things were said in ways that beckoned only the responses of her own thoughts. Ann Jones would bake bread every day and gut the fish that Seifion caught in Bae'r Nant at the north end – things that Gethin never saw his mother do at home. His father spent hours alone reading and meditating; on his first visit to the island, more than thirty years ago, Llŷr had found a sheltered cove near Pen Diben, at the south end beyond the lighthouse. It was to the cove that he retreated, drawn back by the whisperings of Beuno, Dyfrig, Padarn and other long-dead saints, to be with his thoughts and God. Seifion liked to fish for bass and pollack, and in the last years, since his work had taken him to places like Sarajevo and Grozny, he seemed to use his time on Enlli to find some peace inside himself; by the end of the week he'd be lamenting his choice of career in journalism and wishing he could stay. Eilir painted and enjoyed long talks with her mother; but mostly she painted. And for Gethin the island was where wonders unfolded. He watched grey seals and built dry stone walls; he looked, late into the night, for Manx Shearwaters in the beam of a torch and watched for the small flocks of Choughs. Over the years he'd talked with the marine biologists and the botanists, the geologists and the entomologists that stayed at the Bardsey Bird and Field Observatory and accompanied them on their field trips; for Gethin the island was a living encyclopaedia of the natural world.

On the evening before they crossed over to Enlli the whole family had lingered at the supper table. Eilir had unfolded the saga of the last days of the fungus on the kitchen wall and Seifion had told them stories about New York – the unbearable August heat, the congestion and pollution caused by too many cars, the crumbling health care system – about which he'd been doing a piece for his newspaper.... Then Eilir had talked about *her* AIDS patient; Ann had wanted to know if they were using the new combination therapy in Liverpool, the one she'd read about in the *BMJ*. Seifion told the grim details of a visit to an under-funded AIDS hospice, run by a group of nuns in Queens, where people died in their own filth.... Eilir couldn't speak highly enough about the loyalty and care her AIDS patient's partner had shown and how impressed she'd been with the faithfulness of her patient's gay friends. 'Gwrywgydwyr ydy'r grwp sydd mewn perygl o hyd ta – Homosexuals are still the highest risk group then,' Ann had said. Both Eilir and Seifion tried to say something about how it was behaviours that were risky, and that the notion of risk shouldn't be pinned onto groups of people like a badge, but their words were lost as the talk shifted from health care to homosexuality. Llŷr didn't believe that God was punishing homosexuals through this disease, but that the disease was a consequence of their sinfulness and the biggest lesson to humanity from the whole AIDS crisis was that if we chose to flout God's law some pretty catastrophic things would happen.

Seifion talked about two gay friends, one from university days and the other a journalist; coming to know these two men had made Seifion re-think his position – the position he'd grown up with – Llŷr's position. Seifion didn't think, any longer, that being gay was sinful... and wasn't all the work with the human genome project going to reveal that sexual orientation was genetically predisposed? If that was true, then gay people were an intended part of God's creation. Llŷr had said that even if science did reveal the genetic basis of sexual orientation, that didn't make homosexual acts any less sinful; the Bible was clear that sexual intercourse between a man and a woman in marriage was what had been ordained; celibacy was the only acceptable lifestyle for homosexuals, as it was for all unmarried people.

Perhaps Gethin imagined that both his brother and sister had blushed on hearing this; he knew that he'd blushed as soon as they'd started talking about homosexuality. He'd thought that he might clear the table while they talked, to hide his anxiety and embarrassment, and yet, the things which Eilir and Seifion had said had been interesting and positive. Before falling asleep, he decided that he'd talk with Seifion in the morning when they drove together to Porth Meudwy at the tip of the Llŷn.

Waiting on the pebble beach for the two rowing boats to carry everyone and everything bound for the island across the bay to the larger boat in the anchorage, Gethin considered his disappointment. Who was he most disappointed in, himself or his brother? Seifion had said it was a phase that he'd pass through; he'd even shared with Gethin that he and two other boys, when they were about thirteen, had 'played' with themselves and had competitions to see who could do it quickest and shoot highest. When Gethin hadn't seemed convinced, Seifion talked about a sexual experience with a French boy during a language exchange when he was about Gethin's age; they'd

31

shared the same room for the whole of Seifion's stay and done things in bed together; none of it had meant that he was gay. Gethin hadn't tried to explain what he knew to be true; but then – he didn't have the words to give it any shape, and alongside Seifion's experiences Gethin had nothing to share – just an intuitive knowing, without form or outline – without a voice.

Bugail Enlli rounded Pen Cristin and came into calmer water. The sound had been wilder than Gethin could remember and everyone was soaked. The two Germans left behind by the Observatory boat had sat next to him and in the first minutes of the crossing, in the relative calm of the Llŷn's lee, they'd introduced themselves. Gethin, filled with the confidence of his A*, had said, 'Hallo! Mein Name ist Gethin Llŷr.' He'd tried to explain that it would probably get rougher once they got into the channel and that it might be a good idea to wear the waterproofs that were tucked through the straps of their rucksacks. Bernd, the one Gethin supposed was about his own age, speaking in English that was better than Gethin's German, had said that it was his first time on such a small boat. When all the conversations had submitted to awe at the waves and silent prayers, Bernd wove his arm through Gethin's to stop himself being thrown around so much. Later, standing side by side on the uneven jetty in the Cafn, passing all the luggage from the boat along the line to the waiting tractor and trailer, Gethin and Bernd talked easily. The German boy was impressed that Gethin had been to the island every summer; he asked about its wonders. Did Gethin know about the Seal Cave? He'd read all about it; was it hard to find? Gethin said that it was, but that he'd take him there if he liked.

When Bernd came to Carreg Fawr later in the day to find Gethin, Ann Jones, who'd been kneading the first batch of dough, had tried to explain that she wasn't Mrs Llŷr, but Mrs

Jones – but that he could call her Ann anyway. Bernd, in his confusion, had said that in Germany it was impossible for children not to carry their parent's family name. Ann had done her best to explain that her three children were named according to an old Welsh tradition whereby sons were known as 'son of' and daughters as 'daughter of' – so Eilir was Eilir Ann and Gethin was Gethin Llŷr. Though Gethin had gone fishing with Seifion and Ann didn't know for sure when they'd be back, Bernd stayed with her at Carreg Fawr and she told him stories about the island; he especially liked the idea that they might be stuck there for days if the weather turned bad. When Gethin and Seifion returned with three large pollack, more than enough for supper, Bernd and Gethin went to climb all five hundred and forty-eight feet of Mynydd Enlli; from the 'mountain-top' Gethin could point out interesting places and give Bernd his bearings.

The hour after all the supper things had been cleared away was quiet time. Gethin had never thought to question this, it was part of their life on Enlli; an hour in silence to listen for the wisdom of the twenty thousand saints and God. The last quarter of the quiet hour was evening prayer and they all came together in the small front room; sometimes this was silent too, and at other times someone would say whatever their day on the island moved them to say. Gethin thought about Bernd; when he'd put his arm through Gethin's, on the boat, he'd become aroused... he'd had an erection. The memory of it, now – before God, left him filled with shame. It would be hard to live as a homosexual in a world with God, Gethin thought, but how much harder might life be without God?

Eilir and Gethin were eating breakfast when Bernd turned up at Carreg Fawr. 'Today we explore the Seal's Cave, ja?' he'd asked. 'Wenn du willst,' Gethin had said, 'if you like!' They put some bread and cheese in Bernd's rucksack and set off to explore the east side of the mountain. Ann shouted after them that they needed to be careful on the sheer slopes above the sound; the last thing she wanted was to scramble on the scree to tend broken legs!

From high up on the north side of the mountain Gethin spotted Seifion, fishing from a shoulder of rock in Bae'r Nant way off below them. As they came over to the east side they saw a man sunbathing; he mumbled something about being careful on the narrow paths. Across Cardigan Bay, Cader Idris proved a worthy throne for its mythical giant and the blue of the sea was spotted with bright sailcloth. When the path dropped away steeply, Bernd betrayed the first clue that the expedition was more dangerous than he'd anticipated: 'You're sure this is the right way, Gethin? If we fall here then – das isses!' Gethin reassured him and suggested that they ease themselves down the steep, scree path on their bottoms. After ten minutes they reached Seal Cave.

Bernd looked disbelievingly at Gethin.... 'But this hole... it's too small... you're sure this is the place?' Gethin remembered that he had thought the same thing that first time with Seifion. 'It's just the entrance that's small, then it opens out....' And Gethin disappeared into the blackness with, 'Come right behind me. You can hold on to my leg if you're frightened....' And then he felt the German boy's hand around his ankle. Half way along the pitch-black tunnel Gethin heard the wheezing and snorting of the seals echo from the underground chamber. He whispered into the darkness behind him that if they stayed as quiet as possible they wouldn't scare the seals. When they both finally pulled themselves from the tunnel onto the wide, flat rock and looked down into the cave, well-lit from a large jagged opening just below the water's surface, they saw two seals basking on the rocks just feet away and another deep in the water, an outline against the water-filtered light. They hardly dared to breathe and marvelled at the wonder of it all.

After ten, perhaps fifteen minutes, Bernd had asked, in a whisper, whether they could swim with the seals. Gethin remembered that he and Seifion had swum in the cave a few times, but that the seals were usually frightened off. 'We can try....' Gethin whispered back. Bernd stood up and as he took off his clothes Gethin saw that his body was already that of a man. 'Come... let's swim,' he whispered, beckoning Gethin to undress. Gethin followed him into the water. The two basking seals snorted, wriggled from their rocks and dived deeply, circling them both before making for the under-water exit to the open sea. The boys were enthralled and hugged one another, each discovering the other's excitement. They swam together... touching... exploring one another's bodies.... And they kissed. On the wide, flat rock above the water they lay in one another's arms for a long time, their bodies moving together. Bernd's sigh, when it finally erupted from somewhere deep inside him, echoed around the cave before dying away into Gethin's low moan.

During the quiet hour that evening Llŷr told them the story of Saint Beuno and the curlew; he'd watched the birds for most of the afternoon, breaking off the legs of small crabs before swallowing them. According to the legend, Beuno, in the years before coming to Enlli to die, had lost his book of sermons overboard on a stormy sea crossing; in some despair, he arrived back at his cell in Clynnog Fawr to find his sermons, pulled from the sea and carried back to him by a curlew. It was a story Gethin had heard every summer on the island, but then, of Enlli's twenty thousand, Beuno was his father's favourite. Gethin's mind wandered to Bernd and to Seal Cave and now, before God, he wasn't so sure that it was the 'beautiful thing' it had been that afternoon.

35

Later, feeling heavy with a guilt that only Welsh Calvinism could bestow, Gethin left Carreg Fawr in search of some distraction. Near Ogof Hir he looked for Shearwaters. Beuno came to him.... And then there were two others, perhaps Dyfrig and Padarn, but their faces were hidden under their hoods... and there were curlews; lots of curlews. Startled by the swiftness of their appearance, Gethin dropped his torch; the glass broke as it hit the rocks and the beam died. The blackness of the night wrapped itself around him and, through the curlew's melodic 'curlee', Beuno whispered his wisdom. Gethin didn't want to hear words of judgement and condemnation and he hit out at the three robed figures, shouting at them to leave him alone. Their robes and whisperings folded over and under him and, quiet in their embrace, he was carried back to Seal Cave. Beuno spoke through the whisperings of the other two in a babble of Latin and Welsh, Greek and Hebrew, and though it sounded odd, Gethin understood. Beuno wept for all the men down the centuries whose lives had been tortured by self-hatred because they had loved other men. 'The glory of God is the fully alive human being,' he'd said, 'and as it is your providence to love men, love them well, in truth and faithfulness.... Where love is true and faithful, God will dwell.... *Ubi caritas et amor, Deus ibi est....*'

The bell rang and as Gethin watched Mr Bateman pack away his books he decided that his need to talk might keep until another day. They both reached the library door together and with a broad smile, Mr Bateman asked, 'Sut wythnos ges ti ar Enlli? – What sort of week did you have on Bardsey?' Gethin said he had a lot to tell and agreed to help set up some apparatus in the lab during the lunch break. And so Gethin got to talk.

Mr Bateman listened as Gethin explained that he now realised he was gay and understood that he needed some support, but he interrupted Gethin when he started to tell him about Bernd and the Seal Cave.... 'I don't want to know if you've had sex with boys, Gethin; that would put me in a difficult position.' And he explained about the school's policy on sex education and the laws that guided it; 'I'd be expected to inform the head if I knew that one of our pupils was having sex below the age of consent... and the school policy doesn't really give me much guidance on how to talk with you about gay issues.... Can't you talk about this with someone else?' After a long silence Gethin said that he didn't think there was anyone else, but that he didn't want to put Mr Bateman in a awkward position either, and he left the lab feeling let down and lonely.

That evening, when the loneliness became too deep, Gethin told his parents he was gay. Ann said she'd ring one of the psychiatrists at the hospital. Llŷr knew of a healing ministry on the Wirral that had some success in saving homosexuals. They both wanted the best for him. *Ubi caritas et amor, ubi caritas, Deus ibi est.*

Later that evening Kevin Bateman talked with his brother's lover, David, about what support he might offer Gethin; 'You could suggest that he phone the gay help-line in Bangor....' He then wrote Gethin a note to say that he was sorry for letting him down and he put the phone number David had given him clearly on the bottom. *Ubi caritas et amor, ubi caritas, Deus ibi est.*

But Names will Never Hurt Me

The seagulls have already been squealing for an hour or more. You give in to your restlessness and lie, wide-awake, in the damp, tangled sheet trying to identify the different birds by their calls. The herring gulls, by far the commonest on your stretch of coast, bark their deep kyow-yow-yow while the lesser black-backed gulls' more throaty ow-ow-ow-kyoww offer the chorus in the dawn concert. There are rasping kierr-inks of sandwich terns and the fast, chattering kirrikiki of little terns. You remember the afternoons you spent with Deio-flat-fish on the quayside learning these strange bird voices. You'd been much younger then and your world hadn't seemed so complicated.

They'd started calling you names even before it had dawned on you. You wondered sometimes, if it hadn't been for the name-calling, whether you would even have thought about it. You'd known that there were people like that, in the worlds of soap operas, television personalities and big cities, but your little piece of Welsh coast seemed so untouched. Of course there were the holidaymakers and their antics, but they came and went. The first time they'd called you *bum-boy* you hadn't really understood what they'd meant; then it was *shirt-lifter*, and that one had really baffled you too. *Effing queer* was much more straightforward, even if you couldn't understand why they were calling you that. But then, as the months passed, you came to recognize in yourself what others had already seen. It was unspeakable.

By the time the name-calling had become a daily event, the name-callers had grown bored and dissatisfied by your apparent indifference to their taunts and they'd begun to push you around. In the changing rooms before and after games they flicked their towels at you. One day they even forced your head into the toilet bowl while two of the boys pissed on it and another flushed the toilet. Everyone was laughing when Mr Jones, the games teacher, came to see what all the commotion was about; he'd laughed too. You had thought many times about telling your mam, but how could someone talk about the unspeakable?

You couldn't tell when you'd actually started to believe you were a bad person; perhaps it had been during those months when none of your *friends* would let themselves be seen with you. You'd spent lots of time on your own then and all the bad names they'd called you seemed to get inside you. Was it then that you'd been with the boy in the toilet by the golf course? You don't remember the sequence of events now, but you do remember how dirty you'd felt afterwards. You can still recall the smell of the greasy haired youth's sweat, the taste of the white scum under his foreskin and the stale urine stench in the uncared-for public toilet. After that it wasn't just the bad names under the skin that made you feel bad.

There had been many boys and men after that first time. Despite all the promises you made to yourself never to do it again and the desperate prayers to have such feelings taken away, you let yourself be pulled into the game again and again. First the eyes would catch the gaze of another and linger; they were always holidaymakers, playing such games with locals would be too dangerous. After stares that seemed to loiter there would be quiet smiles and perhaps a nod of the head, then one or the other would lead the way into a public toilet where you'd stand for longer than was possible if it had been just for a pee. When each was confident of the other's intention – a kind of knowing that you came to understand and which became more certain with experience – a place would be negotiated; a tent or a beach hut, even the rocks and caves at the bottom of the cliffs. Caravans were best of all because the curtains could be drawn and the door locked. Failing these options, and if you both were desperate enough, it would be in a toilet cubicle against walls smeared with lurid messages and cartoon phalluses.

Sometimes, when you let yourself remember, the shame suffocated you. At such times you tried to recall what legacy these liaisons and encounters left you to be grateful for. Sex education at Ysgol-y-Traeth, its curriculum barely discussed by the embarrassed, middle-aged, respectable chapel-goers on the governing board, had failed to acknowledge the real world of AIDS and unplanned pregnancies. It was these men and boys, in holiday shorts and suntan cream, who'd taught you about using condoms and safer sex. Some had even shown tenderness.

Others had been brutish, especially in the days of your inexperience, taking what they wanted by threat or by force... Not that you'd ever been beaten up... You'd never had to lie about a swollen lip or a black eye. Even those who'd said *yes* to your *nos* hadn't been violent in that sense; they'd just held you down more firmly than was comfortable and pushed harder. You'd soon learned that clenching the muscle as tight as possible only made it hurt more so your *no* was usually interpreted as a *yes* because you relaxed to save yourself the pain. After learning about KY or using loads of spit, with the boy from Wolverhampton – the one you'd seen every day for a fortnight because you'd liked one another, it became easier and more convenient to say *yes* even though you never liked it. And so any possible nastiness had been avoided.

The alarm clock ringing out from your parents' bedroom breaks through the thoughts and the seagulls. Your attic bedroom, with sloping ceilings and sea view, is still stifling from the previous day's heat. The white tee-shirt you'd worn the night before, stained at the armpits, is lying over the back of a dining chair that looks curiously out of place next to the small chest of drawers. On the chest, amid the clutter of deodorant cans, after-shave bottles and tubes of creams for spots and athlete's foot, the two ten-pound notes are where you left them. You try again to remember a forgotten errand or any other reason why they should have been in the back left-hand pocket of your jeans. You don't want to accept that the slightly drunk American with the snake tattoo coiled around his thigh, its head questioning at his pubic hair, must be the source of such munificence. Twice you'd told him that you didn't take money and that as long as he used a condom with plenty of lube you didn't mind. He must have put the two notes into your pocket when you went to the toilet in the cramped camper van after you'd had sex. You wonder why the snake man had felt the need to pay for something you'd been willing enough to give.

As you shower that sunny August morning of your seventeenth birthday, you think about all the hurtful names you've ever been called. There'd been *effing queer*; there'd been *turd-driver* and *arse-bandit*. *Rent-boy*, though, didn't sound so bad.

41

My Velvet Eyes

Prysor Lewis lay, still and shrunken, in a tangle of tubes and wires. After some time staring at the bedside monitor, fascinated by the peaks and troughs, Sam could recognise none of the feelings he thought a son might have at a father's deathbed. He'd even found himself fantasising about Frank, his father's nurse, wondering if the three studs in his left ear were an indication that there may be other pierced bits under his uniform. Slouched in a chair at the dying man's side, his arms folded across his chest, he tweaked the nipple rings through the cotton of his tee shirt unconsciously and thought about what sex with Frank might be like.

After some time, he wondered what Sawel Rhys would have felt. Maybe hurt and anger at his father's rejection? But Sam's invention of himself had so displaced Sawel that he couldn't reinvent the mindset of his former self. He remembered his father's pronouncement: 'A gay son is as good as a dead son!' Obediently Sawel Rhys Lewis, that timid little Welsh son, had let himself wither away. Sam Rees, young gay man about town, had taken his place. No more Welsh novels, Welsh rock or S4C for Sam; he was into Manchester pink politics and HIV support networks. And when Prysor had excluded him from his own mother's funeral, Sawel had allowed himself to be buried with her.

He was only at the hospital now because of his sister Jane. Adrian had tried to dissuade him from backing out of their planned walking trip, but four kids under ten, a three hundred mile journey with snow in the Borders, and a husband on a business trip abroad had made it hard to argue with her. She'd get there when she could.

When Sam had arrived at the hospital the Charge Nurse in ITU had taken him to one side and warned him gently of Prysor's grave prognosis. Despite the antibiotics they were pouring into him the septicaemia seemed to be knocking out all his vital organ functions, one by one. He'd cautioned Sam of the peculiar contrasts of his father's state, combining periods of lucidness with confused babble and total lapses of consciousness. But it was only when the regular lines skipped out of their pattern, breaking the screen's mesmerising grip on Sam, that he realised he couldn't remain a passive observer at his father's mute death bed. The old man had returned.

Prysor Lewis, oblivious to his son's presence, began to speak. He admonished a patient for inadequate flossing and asked the nurse to mix an amalgam: forever the dentist, he'd returned to his surgery... But then, to Sam's incredulous ears, he began to speak in Spanish. 'Rubén, Rubén,' he called. 'Ot-ra-vez, Rubén... ot-ra-vez... dam-ef-uego.' The words were meaningless to him, apart from scattered Welsh and English references to newspapers and 'the big scandal', but he jotted them down, noting in particular a phrase repeated endlessly by his father, 'Mi-soch-os-de-ter-theo-pelo'.

Adrian wasn't home. Sam absently scanned his note suggesting that they might meet at the gym and moved quickly on to check the answering machine. He heard Jane's voice and Prysor was dead. Through her tears Sam grasped her suggestions for meeting up with him to sort out death's practical aftermath. He dialled her number but the phone rang out; she'd put her plans into action and was on her way.

Untouched by the news of Prysor's demise, Sam remembered that he and Adrian had planned to be away for the week. He stared into the empty fridge and decided to do a shop; Adrian would have to eat if he decided not to go with them to Wales and he and Jane would need to take some stuff with them... He realised that the decision to stay with Jane in Dolgellau, sorting out Prysor's affairs and arranging the funeral, had already been made. The ghost of Sawel Rhys had nudged his conscience too sharply for Sam to leave these matters entirely to his sister.

Adrian didn't know what to think when he saw Sam sprawled out on the living-room floor surrounded by bags of shopping and the voice of Welsh hymns washing over him. But then he saw Sam's tears and he knew well enough. Adrian lay with Sam, hugging him for a long time, kissing the back of his neck and stroking his hair. Some time later the tears ran dry.

Jane was exhausted. She introduced little Euan Crawford Sinclair to his uncles; he'd cried all the way from Carlisle! Remembering that the hospital had also referred to his sister as Crawford, Sam puzzled over this addition to their names, but as he hugged Jane and her own tears flowed again, Prysor's death took their thoughts in other directions.

Later in the evening their conversation took an enigmatic turn when Jane tentatively announced, 'There's an addition to the family that I haven't told you about... No – I'm not pregnant! But hold on to your seat or this might blow you away.' The family had always believed that Jane's mother had died when she was eleven months old, Prysor later marrying Sam's mother. But Jane told a very different story: Margaret Crawford Lewis, her mother, wasn't dead. 'She spent nearly twenty years in prison, convicted of the murder of her lover, Rubén Ibarruri!'

Jane explained that the Crawfords were wealthy Scottish

landowners, and whilst they'd seen to it that Margaret was living comfortably, they'd also paid some clever lawyers to skip over her in the line of inheritance. About two or three years ago they'd written to tell her that she would become a very rich woman one day, the only condition being that she and her children carried the Crawford name.

'And Margaret?' Adrian asked, 'Have you met her?'

'Oh yes,' Jane smiled, 'many times. She's lovely, but...' And she held Sam's hand across the table, '...but Eluned was our mother.'

'This Rubén... Spanish, was he?' Sam asked, recalling Prysor's delirium.

'Yes... From the Basque country. Don't you remember seeing photos of him in one of the old albums in Cefn Llwyd? He was a dentist, too; he studied with dad in London and they shared a bed sit.'

Sam shook his head.

'Why did Margaret kill him, do you know?' Adrian asked.

Jane bit her lip and after a long sigh she got up from the table. Walking to one of her bags, which was still in the hall, she said:

'I think we'd better open the bottle I brought you both; it's not an easy story to tell and it may even be a harder story to hear.'

She put the Glenfiddich on the table and Sam reached for some clean glasses. But as Adrian began to pour, Euan started crying in the spare room.

While Jane was upstairs feeding the baby, Sam and Adrian cleared the table, washed the few dishes and wondered, over the Glenfiddich, why Margaret had killed her lover and what kind of wealth Jane might be coming into. When she still hadn't returned after nearly twenty minutes Sam went looking for her. She and Euan were sound asleep. A little later, before sleep overtook Sam, Adrian said to him:

'I hope I'm not going to lose Sam Rees... He's the man I fell in love with. That boy who was talking in Welsh to his sister in our kitchen earlier tonight... Who was he?'

Sam held Adrian in his arms until he slept.

They got to Dolgellau late the next afternoon. Jane had been business-like and efficient dealing with the paper work at the hospital in Wrexham, which was more than could be said for the hospital staff that they dealt with. She and Sam were grateful that Euan had taken so well to Adrian; they'd gone off for a walk in the winter sunshine and discovered a beautiful old walled garden ablaze with crocus, Lenten roses and fair maids of February that Adrian assumed had probably been a part of an estate that the new, sprawling hospital had devoured. Among Prysor's few belongings, handed over to Jane at the hospital, they found a bunch of keys that they trusted would let them into Cefn Llwyd.

Turning up the drive to the old house Jane asked Sam to stop the car.

'I want to say something about Prysor's estate,' she said, reaching into her bag for the bunch of keys she'd been handed in the hospital. 'Here, you take these.'

She pushed her hand through her hair and turned in her seat so that she could also see Adrian in the back with Euan and with some hesitation she said:

'This all may be a bit premature because I don't know anything about Prysor's will... I know that we're all the family he had and that he didn't have anything to do with you two, so it would seem likely that he's cut you out...'

'There's no need for this, Jane,' Sam interrupted, tossing the keys gently into her lap.

'Sam, let me finish,' she said and sighed. 'I don't know what we'll find in his sock drawers or under the mattresses, but whatever he's left to me, I'll get our solicitor in Edinburgh to transfer it to you.'

'No Jane, don't do this,' Sam said, shaking his head, 'he doesn't owe me anything and I've got no expectation that I'm included. I'm here to support you. Isn't that right, Ady?'

'No...' Adrian searched for words and waved his hands, 'don't bring me into it. This is one of those times I'm grateful that the law doesn't recognise our marital bliss. This has got to be between the two of you.'

A silence fell heavily over them. Adrian tried to lift them out of it: 'You've got to admit though Sam, the house would make a lovely gay B & B. I bet we'd make a bomb with all those butch mountaineers from the Gay Outdoor Club. We could do all the exterior paint-work pink and advertise in *Gay Times*.'

They all laughed and Sam drove on to the house.

Even before they'd emptied the car a neighbour turned up, a bottle of milk and a loaf of bread in her basket. Before they sat down to eat that evening four other callers had paid their respects and left them with an apple tart, a Victoria sponge, a dozen fresh eggs collected that day and a basket of winter vegetables. Adrian, who'd lived all his life in various Manchester suburbs, had never witnesses that kind of pulling-together in a community. Jane sat at the large oak table in the kitchen feeding Euan while Sam cooked. Their conversation had lapsed and Jane spoke sweet nothings to the baby at her breast.

'What was that you said to Euan?' Sam asked.

'Oh... It's just something Margaret says to him... I'm not even sure I pronounce it properly.'

'Say it for me, Jane.' It was almost a command.

She looked curiously at her brother and said:

'It's something like *Mis ojos de terciopelo*.'

'What does it mean, Jane?' Sam asked sharply.

'I don't know exactly; it's something like 'my velvet eyes'. It's just one of those sweet things you say to babies... Or to your boy or girlfriend. What's the matter, Sam? Tell me.'

'When I sat with Prysor yesterday morning he was quite delirious and that was one of the things he kept saying.'

'Oh, I see... Well, like I said, it's one of Margaret's sayings. Perhaps it's something she used to say to him.'

'Sure, that makes sense, I suppose,' Sam said, turning back to the Aga which he still hadn't quite got the hang of.

It was Sam, after they'd eaten, who finally suggested that they look for Prysor's papers. Adrian volunteered to wash the dishes but Jane was anxious that they went through things together. They found his desk orderly and its contents mostly filed neatly away in clearly identified folders; buildings insurance, utilities, BT & gas shares, bank statements, credit card accounts, car... An old wallet contained a wad of £20 notes. Jane counted the money and handed it to Sam, who gave it back to her and said they'd better look for a copy of the will so that they'd have some idea what to do with it. Adrian found some old photographs, wrapped carefully in a paper bag and held together with an elastic band. Jane looked through them and recognised Margaret in her wedding gown; another was of the wedding party:

'Wasn't Prysor handsome when he was young?' she said, pointing him out to Adrian.

'Hmm... His brother was pretty cute too; was he the best man?' Adrian asked.

Jane looked at the man he was pointing to:

'Oh... That's Rubén Ibarruri; he was their best man. It's funny, until you mentioned it I never realised how much alike they were. Look Sam...' she said, passing the photograph to him.

Adrian poured the contents of another envelope onto the hearthrug:

'These are old club membership cards going back years and... Cor... Look at this. A blood donor book with little stamps inside it for every donation he made; he was 'AB'. What are you Sam?'

Jane made a low moan and pushed her fingers through her hair.

'Is this too much for you Jane?' Sam asked. 'Would you rather leave it until tomorrow?'

'I'm 'O',' Jane said quietly; 'my blood group is 'O'.'

'No Jane. Not if dad was 'AB'. You can't be Group 'O',' Sam corrected her.

'I'm 'O',' she said determinedly. 'Margaret knew it all along. She told me, you know, the second time I met her. I thought she was just being mischievous; that twenty years in jail had made her bitter. She told me I was Rubén Ibarruri's daughter... But honestly, I didn't want the proof of it. Prysor was my dad. But here we have it; all the proof we need.'

She picked up the little book filled with stamps, and she wept. Both Sam and Adrian held her for a long time.

Much later, after they'd drunk a few glasses of Prysor's Laphroaig, Adrian said:

'None of this really makes sense to me. Why did Margaret kill Rubén Ibarruri if they were lovers and she knew him to be your father?'

'He took another lover,' Jane said.

'God... That's a bit over the top, isn't it?' Adrian quizzed. 'I mean, killing him just because he found another woman. She was married after all... He was only doing to her what she was doing to Prysor.'

'Rubén's new lover was a man and that made Margaret angry as well as jealous.'

And Sam heard Prysor calling out for Rubén: *Mis ojos de terciopelo.*

The Magenta Silk Thread

Mrs Amelia Roberts had waited on the platform for the eight eighteen to Shrewsbury for a good ten minutes before the train pulled in. The wind, which came right through the town off Cardigan Bay, carried a light drizzle, and in the fifteen-minute walk to the station from Prince of Wales Crescent it had left her feeling chilled; through her Aquascutum raincoat and navy Viyella suit she felt the dampness niggle the rheumatic in her hip. She'd thought of phoning for a taxi when she'd pulled back the heavy velvet curtains of the front sitting-room bay window and seen the overcast seascape, but Cader Cabs had let her down twice before. Run by a local boy, too. It was a shame he was so unreliable; with that rough crowd from the Midlands moving in and buying up everything, she liked to support the few locals still in business, but... While she was generous enough to give people the opportunity to make amends, no one ever got a third chance with Mrs Amelia Roberts.

It hadn't occurred to her that at seventy-seven the trip to Shrewsbury might be too much for her. She couldn't remember the last time she'd taken the train; for years now, if she'd wanted to go shopping for clothes, or even just fancied a day out to Chester or Llandudno – or that nice Cheshire Oaks place in Ellesmere Port, she'd go in the car with Megan *Paris House,* always making sure she paid for their lunch and half the petrol. But this time she'd said nothing to Megan; as well as they both knew one another, she wasn't sure what her friend would make of it all. This occasion was different... Yes, a very different kind of event – and very special, and she didn't want anything that Megan might say to spoil it. Taking the train saved Amelia Roberts from having to explain.

She'd never liked crossing Barmouth Bridge on the train; when the tide was high and the wind blew in off the sea, the windows would be splashed by the waves and it was all too unnerving... And since those worms had been eating away at the wooden piles she'd decided the bridge probably wasn't safe anyway, despite all the thousands of pounds British Rail had paid to repair it. As the train pulled slowly out over the swollen estuary she willed herself to think about something pleasant for the next five minutes; after that she could relax and enjoy the countryside.

It was her Jack's smiling face that came to her: fresh and freckled, his green eyes ablaze under all those foxy curls. They were dancing; one of the regular Saturday night dos in the assembly room with the local third-rate dance band playing all the songs from *Top Hat* and *Follow the Fleet* (that had just shown in the White Cinema) led by Eddie Jones; despite blackheads and dirty fingernails from shovelling in the coal yard, he sang *Cheek to Cheek* thinking he was every girl's answer to Fred Astaire. She felt Jack squeeze her to him as they moved across the dance floor; in her Jack's arms she wondered about the things that never were because of those German bullets on a beach near Boulogne. Their years of married life together. Their children growing up and having families of their own. How well Jack would have aged with those high cheekbones and how he would have enjoyed their grandchildren. None of it hurt like it used to. Was that because old age had brought her wisdom or had her heart just hardened after fifty-eight years a widow? She was just glad that it had stopped hurting. Had anyone been sitting opposite Mrs Amelia Roberts as the train crossed over the estuary bridge, they may have seen the fingers of a gloved hand dance on the arm-rest to an inaudible rhythm and perhaps glimpsed the quiet smile on a face that looked at peace with the world.

When the train pulled away from the coast in its faltering dash across Montgomeryshire towards Newtown, the late summer countryside emerged from the clinging shroud of coastal mizzle and the bright sunshine enlivened the land's fading colours. Mrs Amelia Roberts' face flushed, though no one sat close enough to notice, as she remembered that she'd left the chamber under her high brass bed with the previous night's two offerings unemptied. She wondered, if fate were to play some cruel tricks on her that day, a train disaster or a heart attack, what Betty-next-door would think when she took her spare key and began to rummage. And she laughed to herself when she thought about the other little treasures Betty might find that would make the piss pot seem incidental.

Thinking about Betty-next-door made her think about Nellie Bet, who, in turn, made her think about Glyn. It was for him she was making the effort; buying a new rig-out when she had a wardrobe full of Jaeger and Viyella. It was a shame that Nellie Bet hadn't lived to see it; she'd done nothing about that diabetes for years and in the end she'd just let herself go until the gangrene was stinking... But then, had she lived, none of it would be happening in quite the same way and she wouldn't have been sitting on the train going to Shrewsbury. Of course she'd missed Nellie Bet these past eighteen months; they'd known one another all their lives... It was she who'd told her, after the telegram, that she had to get on with her life...

'Milli', she'd said, 'War is war and your Jack's dead. You don't owe it to him to be a mourning virgin for the rest of your life.'

But what she'd given to her Jack she couldn't give to anyone else and despite many an overture it was as Mrs Jack Roberts she'd remained, until, hardly without noticing, Jack was forgotten by most of the town's folk as they took to calling her Mrs Amelia Roberts.

Nellie Bet never forgot. She always made sure that 'Our Milli' was part of her family; matron of honour at her wedding, godmother to Lois and Griff, and always expected for Sunday dinner and Christmas Day. And then, when Glyn had come along, a real after-thought at forty-two, Nellie Bet took to leaving him for hours on end with her in the shop. The summer visitors who came to Morgan's Woollens to buy hand-knits and yarns, and skirt lengths from the mill in Trefriw, knowing no better, used to think she was his mother. Even if she did sometimes secretly think of Glyn as her own child, as Nellie Bet's gift to her, Amelia Roberts had never claimed him as her own.

Certainly she'd wiped Glyn's bottom, fed him *Ostermilk* and burped him more times than Nellie Bet had ever done. She'd read him stories and helped with his homework, and taken him on his first visit to Chester Zoo because he wanted to see real elephants. It was to her he'd come to be tutored in his recitations for all the different local eisteddfods because his Mam had said that Anti Mill had got more patience, and she'd taken him to the Dragon Theatre to see summer shows, pantomimes and Gilbert and Sullivan. Hadn't it been the comfort and reassurance she offered, not his mother's, that Glyn had sought when there were crises in his life? Like the time after he'd fallen from the rocks near Tŷ Crwn (playing best-for-dying a bit too earnestly), his fractured leg held stiff in plaster of Paris for two months. He'd stayed the whole time with her, and when he'd got bored with jigsaws and reading she'd taught him to knit after he'd become fascinated by the cables and diamonds that hung from her needles... And it was to her he'd come, straight from the train in the first weeks after he'd gone to the secondary school in Harlech all bloodied and crying after the Penrhyn boys had taunted and punched him because he was a sissy.

Mrs Amelia Roberts' daydreams were disturbed when a fat, red-faced woman with a cod's mouth and eyes more bloodshot than a bulldog's squeezed onto the train in Caersws and sat opposite her across the narrow table. She smelled the rich mixture of the hill farm this country woman had left earlier somewhere deep in the folds of the hills, and Amelia Roberts remembered the goats she and Nellie Bet had herded when they were land girls. How they had both hated those goats for the way their smell clung. The cod-mouthed woman rummaged in a shopping bag and pulled out her knitting. Amelia Roberts watched the stout, fleshy fingers loop the five strands of coloured yarn dextrously around the needles in a complex sequence and she envied the woman's skill; Fair Isle had always defeated her. At Newtown the knitting was bundled back into the shopping bag. As Amelia Roberts watched the goat woman's abundant buttocks swagger along the platform into the obscurity of the station's gloom, she dabbed some *Je Reviens* onto her lace handkerchief and patted it around her neck; the perfume masked the smell and awakened some sweeter memories.

The two boys who got on the train with their mother in Welshpool needed a good hiding for the way they answered back the plain, tired-looking woman. Mrs Amelia Roberts had never heard such cheek, not even from the rough fairground crowd who descended on a winter-weary Barmouth in the days before Easter, livening the place up until their departure just before the October gales. The more brazen of the two boys reminded her of Glyn at twelve or thirteen... Not that Glyn had ever been impudent; it was something in the boy's face, a winsome questioning look every now and then. It was just the way Glyn had looked when he'd asked her about wet dreams. That was one of the few times she'd thought to herself, 'He ought to be talking to his father,' but then, what a good-for-nothing Idris *Greenbank Cottage* had turned out to be. She'd never understood how Nellie Bet had put up with his womanising all those years. Of course, she knew what wet dreams were. Hadn't she slept in the same bed as her three older brothers until, one at a time, they'd left home as young men to take up their apprenticeships? But knowing didn't give her the words to speak about such things, and even as the sexual revolution went on all around them and the hippies who lived down by the quay were the talk of the town for their orgies on Ynys y Brawd, she thought it more proper to buy the boy a book by mail order from one of the Sunday newspapers. And so she helped Glyn on his way to adulthood with the gift of *Approaching Manhood* and its chapters on self-respect, honouring girls, self-restraint, and the evils of self-abuse. Glyn never asked her about sex and things again; at the time she remembered thinking that the book must have satisfied his thirst for knowledge, but of course, the letter he sent her from Aberystwyth some years later, just after he'd gone there to study, had set her thinking about just how badly she must have let him down.

Mrs Amelia Roberts took a taxi from the station because the hill up to the shops looked much longer and steeper than she remembered. After a freshly cut sandwich and a cup of tea in Sidoli's (and a visit to their conveniences, which were absolutely spotless) she made straight for the Jaeger shop. She'd neither the patience, nor sadly the spirit to walk through Gullet Passage and Grope Lane, or the other eccentrically named streets and alleys that had once fascinated and invited her curiosity about the first Elizabeth's times. The assistant, who wore too much make-up, had been perhaps a little too obsequious with her *madam this* and her *madam that*. But she'd been helpful, and Amelia Roberts left the shop in the knowledge that the suit – a cashmere and wool mix in mulberry, shot with a magenta silk thread that married the blouse – would be delivered after a minor alteration to the jacket, together with a lavishly elegant hat in navy, with gloves to match. Her shopping all done she felt suddenly weary, and walking to the taxi rank she consciously banished the voice that questioned her extravagance.... Her Glyn deserved the best. Back home and walking to Prince of Wales Crescent with the gay music of the fair ground rides cheering even the gloomiest alleys on all sides, Mrs Amelia Roberts, though quite exhausted by her excursion, brimmed with excitement and confidence, for now she knew she wouldn't let the boys down.

Sitting in the bay window of her front sitting room with a cup of tea and a slice of the Madeira cake she'd bought at the Cancer Research sale-of-work, Amelia Roberts wondered what she might say at the service. Robert, who'd taken to calling her Anti Mill after she'd sent him letters and cards during those awful months he was in the hospital, had impressed upon her how much it would mean to them both, and naturally she couldn't refuse him. Of course she understood Robert's mother's discomfort too. Hadn't she tried for years to open Nellie Bet's mind, when she wouldn't even let Robert over the doorstep? Amelia Roberts knew well enough that for as long as people were shunned because they were different, their public acts became acts of defiance; for that very reason, what Robert and Glyn were doing *was* political. She relished the role they'd asked her to play.

After the service, it wasn't Robert that people had talked about for months after, though he'd been movingly presented in his wheelchair by his mother. Nor was it the Minister, Celia, a middle-aged mother of four who'd blessed the men with unpretentious reverence. It was of Amelia Roberts that people spoke, the elegant old aunt, whose words of congratulation, and encouragement for their life together, had been as vivid and precious as the magenta silk thread in her mulberry suit.

Etienne's Vineyard

They sat in the garden, an almost empty bottle of red wine on the lawn between their chairs; it was warm now from the afternoon sun, and neither of them wanted the dregs from the bottle. Lowri wondered about fetching the bottle of white from the fridge, but thought better of it once she'd realised the depths to which Hywel had sunk. When she'd suggested that they drank a glass of wine in the garden she'd thought that the six weeks of school holidays he'd spent in France had done him some good, but now she wasn't so sure.

'This Etienne, then,' she said in her usual mixture of Welsh and English, 'he sounds like a real *cachgi*, an absolute shit.'

'No.' Hywel said, shaking his head. 'No, he's not; he's...' He searched the afternoon heat for some words to describe his French lover, but Marc stole his thoughts.

'He was drop-dead-gorgeous I suppose,' Lowri said, 'with blonde hair and a sun tan? And a big cock? Good in bed, was he?'

Hywel wiped the tears from his eyes and asked, 'What about Marc then? Has he been in touch?'

'Marc?' Lowri's face gave away the bad taste which his name left in her mouth. 'Not a dickie bird, but that suits me. I don't care if I ever see him again.'

'I still love him, Lowri.'

'Oh! Come on, Hywel... We went through all this after he left. He's not worth it.'

'I know it... And I thought he'd stopped haunting me. It was so good to be in France, away from everything that reminded me of him, and after meeting Etienne, and letting myself fall in love again, I thought I was over him. But when I drove back from the airport yesterday, the closer I came to home, the more vividly he came back to me... You just can't stop loving someone because they decided to walk out.'

'No... I suppose that's right, but then, you didn't have to deal with all the deception.'

'Last night, when I was putting the suitcases back in the box-room, I found some of his stuff in a carrier bag; some CDs, a couple of tee shirts, a pair of swimming trunks. I wore one of the tee shirts all evening and listened to his music...'

'So what about this Etienne,' she interrupted, 'how did you leave things with him?'

'He's coming in ten days.'

'Here? To Llan-Aber?'

'I told him that if things worked out for us I'd move to Lyons.'

'But Hywel *bach*, what about your job and the house? What about all those kids who idolise you and end up more fluent in French than in English just because they want to please you. And all the work you've done on the eisteddfod committee, you can't just drop it all.'

She stopped herself saying 'What about me?' but she knew Hywel had heard that too.

'It seemed like a good idea at the time. Etienne asked me if I'd like to live with him and because I thought I'd got Marc out of my system I said that I'd give it some serious thought.'

'But you can't just drop everything here and go'n live in France with some Frenchman you've only known for five minutes,' she said, gripping his arm.

'Until Marc started to haunt me again I didn't think there was much left for me here, but now I'm confused. If I thought for a moment that he'd come back, I'd write to Etienne and tell him not to come.'

Lowri thought again about the chance meeting with Marc's brother at the theatre in Harlech the week before and she changed her mind about not telling Hywel. 'There's been some talk in the village that he's in Bangor. You could call round at his mother's; she might be able to tell you something, an address or a phone number maybe.'

They sat across the table from one another, their half-eaten steaks, pushed around the plates and played with, not enjoyed, as good food should be. Marc drew heavily on his cigarette, 'So, go to France then, if that's what you want.'

Hywel wondered what Marc would need to do to make him hate him enough to feel that he could leave. He looked into those eyes which had so often teased and invited, saying, 'But I still love you, so I'm not free to go.' Marc stubbed out his cigarette with such brutality that his glass of wine spilled, bleeding into the tablecloth. He swore loudly, drawing the unwanted attention of others. The waiter fussed, and as he cleared away some of the clutter that was between them he suggested that if they had finished their meal they might like to move into the bar. Marc, believing that the waiter wanted them out, felt his anger rising, 'Just bring us the bill and we'll go!'

Hywel, pouring salt on to the wine stain, said, 'Lowri really hates you; that's why she's been able to pick herself up and move on. It's not like that for me. I came home one day and you'd gone, and I still don't know why. You still haven't told me why.'

Lighting another cigarette, Marc said, 'She hates me because I started fucking her little brother; it's a good enough reason and the divorce court thought so too.'

'Is that all I was for you, Marc; just someone to fuck? And all that time I thought you loved me.'

'Love? Oh Hywel, you're such a bloody romantic; you've had your head too long in those French novels. Do you know what? I don't think I know what love is.' Then he smiled, and through a puff of smoke he said, 'But I know what good sex is. I know what I like and with you it just stopped being fun.'

'For God's sake, Marc, stop it,' Hywel said, shaking his head. 'You're not that empty. We had nearly three years and I know that it wasn't just about sex.'

Marc leaned across the table, stabbing at the space between them with the cigarette between two fingers, he said, 'You lived in your own fantasy, Hywel; you only ever saw what you wanted to see. Do you want me to tell you how many men I had during those three years? Shall I tell you?'

'You're going to tell me whether I want you to or not, Marc, so just say it.'

And in the moments that they waited for the waiter to return with the bill Hywel listened and felt a knot tighten and strangle him inside. Driving back to Llan-Aber, he wondered if the scream inside him was the same scream that had freed his sister.

Lowri passed him the salad and asked, 'How did you meet him then?' Hywel's face softened as he remembered... He was one of Cécile's friends, someone she worked with at the hospital. He'd come round for dinner on the second night after Hywel had arrived in Lyons; Cécile had thought Etienne might take him to the bars and introduce him to a few people. After dinner they'd walked from Cécile's flat near Place Sathonay, crossed the Saône by the Passerelle Saint-Georges, and wandered through the narrow streets of the old city. They'd sat in a café on the Rue Juiverie, smoked Camels and drunk a bottle of wine from

Condrieu; Etienne explained that he had a house there, in his grandfather's vineyard on the slopes of the Rhône.

'I don't understand how an Englishman speaks such good French,' Etienne had said, laughing.

'But I'm not English,' Hywel corrected, with a trace of irritation. 'I'm from Wales; I speak Welsh with all my friends, and my French is good because I teach it in a Welsh language secondary school.'

'I don't know much about the languages in England,' Etienne ventured. 'This Welsh, it's a dialect, is it?'

'No...' Hywel tried to remain civil. 'Welsh is a Celtic language. It's much older than English.'

'But you do speak English?'

'Not very often, if I can help it,' Hywel answered, and tried to explain something of the sometimes bitter relationship between the Welsh and the English. As they walked back to Cécile's, Etienne asked Hywel if they could meet for dinner the next evening, just the two of them.

Hywel helped Lowri wash up the dinner dishes.

'What did you say he was, a psychiatrist?' she asked, rinsing the glasses.

'Yes,' he answered. 'He works some of the week in a hospital and he teaches at the medical school.'

'Older than you then, is he?'

'Only a year or two.'

'He's not married, is he?'

'No, Lowri. He's not married.'

'So why does he want you to live together?'

'It's not just what he wants; I want it too.'

'So you are lovers then,' she said, tentatively.

Hywel remembered their lovemaking; their last time together, hurried, even frenzied, in the hallway of Etienne's apartment, already late, before they left for the airport... And the first time, at the house in the vineyard, gentle and nervous, taking time to discover and learn what pleased... And all those humid nights in Lyons. He smiled at his sister, 'Yes, we are... And it's wonderful.'

She cried and he couldn't console her.

Etienne found it strange to speak in English with Hywel but Lowri had no French so it was all they had to fall back on when the three of them were together. She'd talked about her painting; how reluctant the British were to spend on an original piece of work; how it wasn't easy to make a living as an artist and how most of the tourists to the area wanted sentimental landscapes, which she reluctantly stooped to when there was nothing in the bank to pay the bills. Over dinner they had drunk two bottles of the Condrieu from grandfather Chosson's vineyard and with coffee, Lowri started drinking the Knockando malt that Hywel had brought her, duty-free. Her tongue loosened by the alcohol, Lowri said, 'After my divorce I don't know what I'd have done if Hywel hadn't helped out... Money I mean. I was so down that I couldn't paint... But you're a psychiatrist, so I don't have to explain things like that to you... How long was it, Hywel? Nearly a year? A bit longer? And with Mam and Dad dead and buried I only had Hywel to turn to.' She gulped some more whisky. 'God... I'm so thankful that they were both in the grave before all that happened,' she spat out, venomously. 'Talk of the village we were... Isn't that right, Hywel? And beyond too... Talk of the bloody county, everyone knowing our business.'

She emptied her glass and poured in some more whisky, 'He did tell you, did he, Etienne? He did tell you that he ran off with my husband... My dear brother and my loving husband... I loved them both and they became lovers and made me a laughing stock! Still... You've paid for it, haven't you Hywel? You've paid dearly for it! And now you, Etienne Chosson,' she said, shaking her head and waving the fruit knife she'd lifted from the table in his face, 'You with your suave and sophisticated French ways and your vineyard... You want to take him away from me... No, Monsieur Chosson,' she whispered, stabbing the knife into an orange in the fruit bowl, 'no! Over my dead body. My sweet little Hywel hasn't finished paying yet.'

They lay in one another's arms in the deep peace that came to them after making love; all Hywel could hear, aside from Etienne's breathing, was the sea folding onto the beach below the house.

'Was she serious?' Etienne asked, breaking into the rhythm of the waves.

'She was drunk, and I'm sorry she behaved so badly.'

'Yes, but does she mean what she says? Is she going to make things difficult for us?'

'I don't know... She knows that Marc had lots of men before and after they were married, but she chooses to believe that I took him away from her, and for that she has never forgiven me... It suits her that way.'

'And does she depend on you for money?'

'Not any more. She's doing all right from the gallery... She doesn't believe that what she's turning out is fine art, but it's commercially successful.'

The waves filled the silence between them and then Hywel said, 'It was the drink talking... She won't be difficult... Let's go to sleep.'

Lowri sharpened her mother's large cloth-cutting scissors and put them in the leather shoulder bag she always took with her everywhere. She knew that they would be out; Etienne had told her how much he was looking forward to their hike over Cader Idris. She let herself in and went directly to Hywel's bedroom.

She'd always liked the view from there, out across Cardigan Bay to the Llŷn and Ynys Enlli; she sat in the window seat, and enjoying the view, she shredded every item of Etienne's clothing. Afterwards she pulled the light, summer quilt off Hywel's bed, and seeing the stains of their lovemaking, she plunged the scissors, through the sheet and deep into the mattress, twice, three times... Four... And more... Again and again until she was exhausted. Then she went home and started to prepare the late supper she'd promised the two boys after their day's hike.

They sat next to one another in the window seat. 'She needs help, Hywel,' Etienne said, hardly able to take it in. 'Someone who can do something like this needs help and they need it soon.'

'I don't know what got into her... I'm so sorry... Look... Of course, I'll pay for new clothes...'

'Damn the clothes, Hywel, they're not important. She's sick. We need to see that she's cared for.'

'No... She's not sick. She's just making me pay. She's trying to turn you against me and send you back to France on your own. In her mind, she's just making things even between her and me.'

'Hywel, believe me, that's sick! What do you think she'll do if I don't go? Is she going to come and shred me, like she shredded my clothes?'

'That's ridiculous, Etienne. She wouldn't hurt anybody.'

'Don't be so sure, my love. Remember that I work with people who do things like this.'

It seemed as though there was blood everywhere. The trail went from the kitchen to the hall and on up the stairs. The mirrors in the bathroom dripped blood and his mother's old cloth-cutting scissors lay in the washbasin stained red. Hywel felt the vomit rising and heaved into the toilet bowl.

'She's in the bedroom,' Etienne said. 'You'd better not go in there...'

'She's dead, then?' Hywel asked, kneeling in his sister's blood.

'Yes... Perhaps she thought we'd come back last night, after we'd found my clothes... Maybe that was her intention; that we find her and get her to a hospital.'

'Or maybe this was her last instalment on my debt for stealing Marc from her.'

Later in the day, the police officer handed Hywel the note that Lowri had left, neatly folded in an envelope bearing his name. He read the few words she'd written in her small, neat handwriting: '*My mother's sons were angry with me, they made me keeper of the vineyards; but, my own vineyard I have not kept...* ' *Take care of Etienne's vineyard!*

Pocket Sprung and Nested

'What about this one then?' Tom asked, the impatience of his tone cutting between them across the cluttered, Saturday morning breakfast table. Realising reluctantly that Tom wasn't going to let it drop this time, Dafydd put down the already dishevelled Travel section, poured himself another cup of coffee, and forced a smile that puffed out his ruddy cheeks above an already greying beard.

'All right,' he said, without much enthusiasm, 'you've got ten minutes to convince me.'

Tom smiled, knowing he'd won the initial assault, but not yet sure he'd win the battle.

'This one's ideal; it's got cashmere and lambswool in the top layer, a woven damask cover, and over fifteen hundred springs nested in individual calico pockets.' It was a month since Dafydd had said he thought their bed wasn't as comfortable as it used to be, and Tom's concern for him was evident in the brochures that littered the table.

'And what does all that sales-speak mean?' Dafydd asked with grudging attention, his thoughts still immersed in the once opulent spa resorts of Central Europe.

'Well, it says here, 'The purest cashmere from Asia.... The softest lambswool from New Zealand.... These natural upholstery materials, which include cotton felt from America's Deep South and horsehair from Europe, are healthier and safer to sleep on. They won't sag....' Now, isn't that exactly what we want? You did say that your side of the bed was sagging, didn't you?'

Dafydd nodded his agreement and unconsciously rubbed the dull ache in the bottom of his back. Tom continued to read from the glossy sales catalogue.

"They won't sag or go lumpy, and they absorb and release body moisture efficiently."

'That's just disgusting at breakfast time, Tom,' Dafydd said, pulling a face. 'I don't want to think about the mattress we sleep on absorbing all that sweat and.... Anyway, I thought that's what mattress covers are for.'

Putting the brochure down and buttering the last crust-free triangle from the toast-rack, Tom's little finger made rapid, comically graceful circles in the air each time he drew the knife across the toast.

'If you ever bothered to strip our bed, my dear,' he chided, 'you'd appreciate why some people put their boxer shorts back on after sex.'

'That's enough!' Dafydd protested. And with the slow dawning of acute embarrassment's possibility, he asked sheepishly, 'Does Mrs Mac ever do the bed for us?'

'As if!' Tom said, raising both hands to his cheeks in feigned astonishment. 'She doesn't even clean the toilet for us, Dafydd.... She's strictly hoovering and dusting so I don't think she'll ever blackmail you. Anyway, every man who screws, sweats and pisses gets stains on the mattress; life's like that, and who'd want any other kind of man, hmm?'

Dafydd shrugged and grimaced, 'You're probably right, but I can't be doing with this kind of talk at the breakfast table. Why don't you just mark the ones in the brochures you think will do for us and I'll have a look later.'

After reluctantly scanning the leaflets and accepting Tom's bribe of lunch in Chester, Dafydd conceded defeat. They were whizzing along the A55 even before the breakfast dishes had been rinsed off and stacked in the washer.

Once they'd declared their interest in the lower end of the up-market ranges the assistant at *Asleep-eezy* followed them around like a sissy's poodle.

'We'd like to take a look on our own if that's all right,' Tom said, echoing her tone of forced politeness. 'We'll come to you if we've got any questions.'

'Oh.... It's no trouble, gentlemen. I'm Mrs Chessington, the senior floor manager,' she said obsequiously. 'I'm here to make sure that you know exactly what kind of bed it is you want, and more importantly, to help you know what you're getting for your money once you've decided. Good beds don't come cheap, gentlemen. Now then,' she said, upping her tone into the bossy range, 'it's a single you're looking for, is it?'

Dafydd searched her powdered face for any hint of malevolence, while Tom countered, 'Actually, no.' And then, with the flair of an opera diva in his movements and defiance in his eyes, he put his arm around Dafydd and said, 'We hadn't thought of moving into single beds just yet, had we darling? We're looking for a five-foot, and it has to be six-foot-six long. I mean – just look at the two of us; a bit tubby for a four-foot-six, don't you think? And it has to be firm,' he said, nuzzling up to Dafydd, 'We both like it firm, don't we, dear?'

'The kings are over on the far wall,' Mrs Chessington sallied forth, gesturing, this time like an air hostess pointing out the emergency exits. 'You might want to think about pocket springs then,' she continued, beckoning them to follow her, 'two ample gentlemen like yourselves.' She paused, smiled a syrupy smile, and coughed, 'Well, you'll need a mattress that will give each of you independent support wherever you need it. Pocket sprung mattresses take up the profile of your body and every time you change your position the mattress will cleverly adjust with you. Do come this way.'

Tom knew that Dafydd wanted to leave the store; he knew, too, that they probably wouldn't buy a bed there, but once he'd started playing with Mrs Chessington the sport was just too much fun to blow the whistle on. Tom put his arm through Dafydd's and ignoring his resistance, pulled him after the saleswoman towards the king-size beds. Dafydd's discomfort grew when he noticed other customers trying too hard not to stare. Mrs Chessington, redoubtable in her olive green two-piece, described how honeycomb nested pocket springs made for a bed that was individually responsive, and how the shock waves generated as one person moved were not transmitted through the bed to disturb their sleeping partner. And like a game-show hostess announcing the star prize, she began the final movement of her sales overture.

'This one is a beautiful example of all the features I've mentioned and the English craftsmanship is outstanding.' She ran her fingers along the mattress and with exaggerated reassurance she said, 'It's a good eight inches deep, with these three rows of hand stitching to secure the outer springs to the border so it stays firm to the very edge. The five foot in this range has 2,346 springs, and the more springs you have, the greater the support and comfort.' Patting the damask covering with its floral motifs, encouraging each of them to feel its luxuriousness, she continued, 'It's an absolutely gorgeous mattress, gentlemen, upholstered with the finest quality cotton felt and 4.6 ounces of hand-teased, long-stranded, black horsehair, blended with 3 ounces of the purest lambswool to every square foot.' Tom nodded his faked mindfulness while Mrs Chessington instructed, 'Now, of course gentlemen, the only way you can know if a bed is right for you, is to lie on it. That's why we put these transparent plastic sheets over the bottom half of the mattresses.' And shifting again into airhostess drill she gestured them both to lay beside one another with, 'This particular manufacturer recommends that you take up your usual sleeping position for between ten and fifteen minutes.' And after the briefest of pauses, in which even Tom was lost for words, she said, 'Think about it, gentlemen. I'll give you a minute or two and I'll see if Mr Morgan is free to assist you further.'

'Come on, let's cuddle up,' Tom said with a smile after she'd left.

'God, don't you think I'm embarrassed enough? You've already drawn more than enough attention to us for one afternoon....'

'Oh, come on Daf. Just keep thinking about your bad back. Just another half an hour, sir, and you'll be the proud owner of a bed that will give you ten years of comfortable, health promoting, restorative, restful sleep.'

'What *did* the two of you say to Mrs Chessington?' A voice rang out musically and they turned to face a ginger haired boy, his freckled face broken into a smile, his even teeth all the more white against the charcoal of his suit. Striking the campest of poses with his arms folded across his chest he continued, 'She's come over all queer and had to have a sit down. Mind you,' he said with a classic limp wristed gesture, 'I did say to her, when we saw you coming in, that she ought to let me see to you; but there we are, that's what seniority and commission does, and the most inappropriate person dives in and ends up upsetting the customers. I'm so sorry if she embarrassed you both.' He thrust his clammy hand out to be shaken with, 'I'm Geoffrey Morgan, but you can call me Geoff.'

'I think it's probably for us to do the apologising,' Dafydd protested. 'Tom did go a bit over the top with her, didn't you dear?'

'Bullshit!' Tom retorted, mirroring Geoff's stance. 'I only gave as good as I got! Anyway, Geoff dear,' he said, shaking the boy's hand, 'why don't you sell us a bed?'

Geoffrey Morgan's impersonation of an airline steward made Mrs Chessington seem like a trainee on a government scheme but it soon became apparent that her tutelage had produced something of a clone.

'This one is a beautiful example of fine English craftsmanship,' he said, running his fingers along the mattress. 'It's a good eight inches deep, and with these three rows of hand stitching to secure the outer springs to the border, it stays firm to the very edge. Just feel how firm it is.'

Now even Dafydd began to play the shopping game as both he and Tom felt the firmness of the mattress edge, nodding their agreement with Geoff's commentary.

'Now,' Geoff said, arms folded across his chest again, his hips swaying slightly, 'you two are going to need a five-foot, aren't you?' They both smiled. 'And probably six-foot-six long?' he asked, his right elbow shifting into his left hand, his chin nestling into the palm of the right one. 'Can't have your toes hanging over the edge now, can we? Let me think now.... This range.... the five foot has got 2,346 springs, and the more springs you have, the greater the support and comfort.' And patting the damask covering with its floral motifs, encouraging each of them to feel its luxuriousness, he offered them again the script which Mrs Chessington had already recited.

Ridiculous though the details were, Tom and Dafydd drank in his attentiveness and savoured it.

'But let me impress upon you, gentlemen,' Geoff's performance had reached its climax, his eyes expressing a message wholly absent from Mrs Chessington's pitch, 'the only way you can know if a bed is going to be right for you, is to lie on it.'

FISHBOYS OF VERNAZZA

The Fishboys of Vernazza

Giacomo's knowing smiles and attempts to engage them in broken English don't entice them to dawdle in the Bar Gioia, not even with all the fidgety-fingered cradling of his crotch, as is the way of so many Italian boys. They know that the hike from Monterosso to Vernazza will take at least a couple of hours so they can't indulge in Giaco's flirting or linger over their sticky pastries and cappuccinos. If they miss the train they'll have to wait another hour and that will certainly mean they'll be cutting it fine. Shôn smiles his cheekiest smile and asks Giaco if he'll be behind the bar later.... And so it's agreed that they'll come back and drink *sciacchetrà* with him after they've eaten dinner.

From the gloomy station building that smells rancidly pissy, the passengers that alight the train spill onto the narrow, sun-soaked promenade. Geraint and Shôn stroll beneath the neatly trimmed oleanders, the leaf cover just thick enough to diffuse the sun's warmth and allow them to feel the autumn's chill. Every now and then, Shôn darts from the purple shadows and leans out over the balustrade to ogle the few dedicated sun worshippers that lie in skimpy trunks on Monterosso's sandy beach. Geraint would like to do the same, but it isn't in his nature to be quite so open about his attraction to other men. Knowing this, Shôn describes the delights that he sees (or just imagines) in clipped, crude morsels:

'Nice ass on that one.... Oh God, there's one over there who's got pecs to die for.... And this one here's got such a packet.' Geraint feigns disdain at the teasing and wonders if Shôn has plans to cop off with some handsome Italian. Then, for a few minutes, he considers his place in Shôn's life, despite promising himself that he wouldn't allow such introspection to spoil their time together.

He doesn't like to think of himself as Shôn's fuck-buddy, though that's how Shôn describes their relationship whenever Geraint tries to pin him down. He considers it such a vulgar term, and so American... and it hardly reflects the reality of their nights together when mostly they just cuddle. He's Shôn's teddy bear really, but Shôn's image of himself is far too butch to allow for such a passive interpretation of their liaisons. Geraint doesn't know how much longer he'll let him continue to shape this part of his life. Monogamy and a joint mortgage on a three-bedroomed semi, preferably with a garden, is what he hankers for... a quiet and secure marriage. But they retain their separate lives, their separate flats, their separate circles of friends, and come together only once or twice a week, and for holidays, because that's what Shôn wants. So Geraint takes what he can get; after all, Shôn is a lot of fun to be with... he's gentle, kind and generous (which tempers the bitchy streak), and when a teddy bear to cuddle is the last thing on his mind, their sex is pretty accomplished. Shôn is the only man Geraint has ever loved. And in four years Shôn has never so much as whispered to Geraint that he loves him.

'What about him?' Shôn quizzes, pulling Geraint back from the edge of pensiveness.

'You're like a dog on heat,' Geraint jibes.

The track ascends quickly through the terraced vineyards, taking them along uneven pathways that crown the dry stonewalls and up crude, steep steps that connect the terraces. The vines have been recently stripped and most have been pruned back ready for the winter, their few remaining leaves blotchy with red and gold. The grapes, the *albarola, vermentino* and the *bosco* wither and wizen in some shady spot, a vital step in the process of turning them into *sciacchetrà*. The trail takes them past isolated huts that defy the precipitous gradients with stubborn sturdiness. Around these now forsaken vinedresser's shelters, clumps of prickly pear rear up like tethered, menacing beasts, to deter the inquisitive rambler from exploring. Where the terraces have been abandoned and recolonised by native heathers and squat pines, the *maquis* has reclaimed the derelict refuges.

Above the vineyards, a sea of white-crested turquoise a thousand feet below them, the path, though obvious enough, is rough. Gouged into the face of the mountain, the original course is obstructed time and again by boulders from rock falls. Where landslides have gashed the sea cliff's contours, haphazard cairns mark an imprecise direction across the rock fields.

'You'd think they'd have put a sign up about the condition of the path,' Geraint carps.

'There was one,' Shôn says dismissively, 'but you've got to have a bit of adventure in your life. Besides, the Australians I was talking to last night when you were reading your book said they'd walked it, and once we've crossed the ridge we get back onto the terraces.'

Where the vines begin again, the descent becomes vertiginous. Geraint stops every few minutes to curse his new varifocals and their tendency to blur the irregular steps unless he looks directly down at his feet. Pausing on a bluff, he takes in the view: Vernazza, hanging on its rocky spit around an almost circular harbour, looks like a child's model village, the pink and lemon and ochre of the tall, narrow, green shuttered houses adding to the toy-like quality. Shôn bounds on ahead and after ten minutes or more, Geraint finds him slouched against a rocky outcrop.

'What do you make of this, then?' Shôn asks, pointing at a carving in the rock face.

'Mermaids,' Geraint quips with delight.

'That's what I thought, but...'

'Right... they're boys!'

'Exactly... three cute mermen. I wonder what it's all about?'

'Probably some local legend,' Geraint shrugs. 'The artist was no amateur.'

'It's good, isn't it?'

They come into Vernazza by a lane behind the octagonal domed church, where washing hangs from clotheslines and spider plants hang low from balconies of potted scarlet cyclamen. They find the small terrace of the Ristorante Belforte at the top of the uneven steps at the end of the harbour wall, just like the fetching older couple they'd befriended on the train from Genoa had described: four tables, decked with pink linen cloths and napkins, polished silver cutlery and crystal glasses that glint in the glorious October sun. Shôn, his scientist's eye trained to observe the merest detail, gestures to Geraint that they should sit, as there's no evidence that the splashes from the waves can reach them. Despite Sol's benevolence since their arrival in the Cinque Terre, Neptune and his sirens have been irritable, the sea choppy... squally even; rough enough for the ferryboats that connect the five villages to have abandoned their erratic schedules and for the smaller fishing boats to have remained at anchor. Waiting for *il cameriere* – the waiter – whom the old queens on the train had said, with the campest affection, was *molto delizioso*, they watch the translucent, azure waves rupture into cascades of glistening diamonds as they fold heavily onto the rocks not ten metres below them.

Between glances at the menu, Shôn takes in his surroundings. Over Geraint's shoulder he has a view of the harbour. The fishing boats, brightly painted in red and blue, are pitched by the swell, their short masts tracing the fingerprint whorls on the harbour cliffs where some ancient sea god's hands once moulded the strata. Wherever the rocks give way to vegetation, agaves cling like stranded starfish. Higher up, between prickly pears and heather, an errant bougainvillea bleeds its loveliness from a deep gash. And he thinks of Geraint, and whether he should commit himself.

With a lyrical *ciao,* the fingers of his left hand indolently sinuous at his crotch, *molto delizioso* interrupts Shôn's reverie.

Shôn studies the boy's felinity as he approaches their table. There's a grace in his movements that pleases the eye and suggests he might be a dancer. His arms, the muscles defined beneath a smooth chestnut shell skin, are strong; the sort that take your breath when they embrace you. The features of his face are more Abyssinian than Siamese, and framed by thick black hair, sleek and worn unfashionably long. His smile, in so proud a face, seems slightly mocking but there's a seductive stealthiness in the charcoal of his eyes that quickens Shôn's pulse. In a fleeting thought, Shôn concludes that Geraint, alongside one so dangerously desirable, is too safe... too dependable, and altogether too tame.

Between them they have enough Italian to recognise that there's a choice of local fish on the menu, but they enjoy the boy's attention and pretend to be stupid Brits abroad, coaxing him to translate *pulpo, totani* and *acciughe*. They ask for octopus and squid with potatoes *alla genovese* and freshly-caught anchovies with lemon. As he writes the order on his pad, Geraint notices the silver ring on the waiter's index finger.

'I've never seen anyone wearing a ring there before,' Geraint says after *molto delizioso* goes back into the restaurant, rubbing the index finger of his right hand between the two end joints.

'It's called the middle phalanx,' Shôn says, a bit like a lecturer in an anatomy class.

'Well... whatever... it's still a strange place for a ring.'

'What's even more strange is the pattern and the figure engraved on it,' Shôn scoffs.

'I didn't notice,' Geraint submits.

The boy returns, places a rustic loaf of bread and a jug of wine on the table, and disappears again through the curtain of corded beads that keeps the flies out.

'It's a merman,' Geraint offers, surprised.

As he clears their table, and just after he's asked if they want an *espresso,* Shôn asks him about the carving on the rock above the village.

'You mean the... fishboys?' he hesitates. 'You call them fishboys in *Inglese*?'

'It's a good enough name,' Geraint quips.

'You been to the *grotta del Diavolo*?'

'The devil's cavern? No.'

'Sometimes, when the sea is *tempestoso*, the fishboys come into the village through the *grotto*, and take away... how you say?' The charcoal embers in his eyes glow. 'They take away the bad boys.'

They laugh at his fishy tale and Shôn, catching his eye, teases, 'And just how bad does a boy have to be to be charmed away by the fishboys?'

'Bad enough that... *lui è desiderabile*,' he says with an inscrutable smile and carries the plates away.

'He's quite a story teller,' Geraint says as the curtain of beads clacks. 'Bad enough that you're desirable indeed!'

'He is pretty desirable,' Shôn quips.

'Yes... and did you see how he hid the ring on his index finger in his hand when you asked about the carving?'

'I wonder,' Shôn muses. 'When he leaned over to pick up the plates his hair fell forward. He's got a strange mark behind his ear, all feathery and reddish-purple... just like a fish's gill.'

They eat ice-creams on the *piazza* that fronts the harbour and then cross into the purple shade and take a narrow street made even narrower by stranded fishing boats, hauled from the sea for repair or a coat of paint. Geraint gawps at the large, ugly fish being laid on the marble slabs outside the *pescheria* by the fishmonger, fresh from his siesta. Shôn gawps at the fishmonger's apprentice, a tall, awkward youth with a cheeky smile. As the boy stands before the open refrigerated display counter arranging rose-coloured fish with golden streaks around a hand-written sign that reads *Triglia,* Shôn thinks that in a year or two, when he's filled out a bit, he won't be unattractive. The boy's hands are bloodstained and scaly and a silver ring glints on the middle phalanx of his right index finger... and when he turns, Shôn makes out the curious purple mark behind his ear. So the boy's potential has already been realised. Further up the street the cobbles are drenched in an arc of sunlight. Enjoying the warmth of the sun they peer into the *grotta del Diavolo*. Shôn wonders if the fishmonger's apprentice and the waiter put up much resistance when the fishboys of Vernazza lured them into the devil's cavern.

After a long shower, Shôn sneaks into bed beside Geraint, rousing him from his nap. They cuddle for a while and watch the sun set in a haemorrhaging sky and then they make love, their crazed delight inspired by their holiday mood, the gorgeous waiter and his fable. As their sex gives way to slumber, Shôn supposes that life with Geraint might be worth a try. Watching the last smears of blood fade into the gunmetal sky, Geraint decides it's time to get off the emotional roller coaster of the half-life he half shares with Shôn.

Later, at the Bar Gioia, Giacomo pours three stout goblets of *sciacchetrà*. The silver ring on the middle phalanx of his right index finger catches the light as he tilts the bottle. They raise their glasses, and swirling the richly amber, slightly viscous wine, they toast: '*Salute!*' Geraint's senses fill with curiosity and cocoa, apricot and Mediterranean herbs. Shôn is aroused by his lusty thoughts for Giaco.

'Is a very good one, no?' Giacomo enquires, his round, cheery face filled with pride. 'Is the one my mother makes... much better than the one you buy in the tourist shop.'

'It is very good,' Geraint ventures, his gaze drawn and held in the questioning blue-green of Giacomo's eyes.

'You want to buy *sciacchetrà* you come see me before you go back England,' Giaco says when he's peered too long into Geraint's confusion.

'We will,' Shôn says stressing the *we*, jealous that Giaco seems more interested in Geraint.

Giacomo returns to their end of the bar after serving a giggly teenage couple.

'Can you tell us anything about the carving in the rock above Vernazza?' Geraint asks.

'We couldn't find anything about it in the guide-book,' Shôn says, competing for attention.

'I don't know,' Giaco says with a shrug. 'I never walked on this path.'

'It has three fishboys, like the one on your ring,' Shôn accuses.

Giacomo holds up his finger and looks, almost seriously, at the silver band.

'Is a very cheap ring from a shop in Spezia,' he says, smiling. 'Is very fashionable to have a ring here,' he adds, rubbing the middle phalanx with his thumb.

For a while, they watch Giaco's every move as he serves more customers further along the bar. A larger than life, blonder than blonde girl sweeps into the Bar Gioia with smiles and *ciaos* for everyone. Shôn observes her carefully and deduces that she's the local transvestite. She rests her ample breasts on the bar and reaches over to kiss Giaco, ruffling his sandy curls with her crimson nailed fingers. Her skirt rises as she stretches. Geraint and Shôn are distracted by her black lace panties, which are too skimpy to hide her fishy tail.

Just Beyond the Buddleia Bush

Shifting the heavy Victorian chaise-longue hadn't been as straight forward as Eurig Dafydd had supposed; it had meant moving the formica topped table and the four mismatched dining chairs, and shoving the Welsh dresser over a couple of feet. He'd had to lift the rug too, because every time he lunged at the chaise it had ruffled and snagged around the carved oak legs. Twice he'd nearly given up and, slumping into the solace of the chaise's worn leather, he'd wondered whether he might not leave the damn thing where it was; where it had stood for twenty odd years because Fflur had liked the view across the strait towards Caernarfon and the mountains. But Fflur wouldn't be coming back to *Cwningar*. She'd settled for the house near Rhos in their quite amicable divorce and taken up with a new boyfriend, some doctor from Chester with an annual membership at an exclusive health club that entitled them both to sun-beds, saunas and squash. No more rambles with a Collins pocket flora for Fflur... no more midnight swims in Malltraeth Bay or beachcombing along Newborough Sands. She'd joined the Cheshire set.

Eurig had always preferred the view from the French window, where the three peaks of the Rivals scraped the sky beyond the acres of dunes and the sea, and where a path, just beyond the buddleia bush, cut its way through the August carpet of thrift and common sea lavender in the dune slacks, leading to the secluded beaches near Abermenai Point. With a final shove, he repositioned the chaise and from this new vantage point, lying on the cool leather to catch his breath, he watched two peacocks and a common blue in a complicated dance around the butterfly bush. After some time, the equally intricate moves of two boys, cruising one another as they made for the beach along the path, absorbed his attention. One of them reminded him of Seimon, and lest he should feel again the stab of his oldest son's words, he sought to distract himself and attended to the rug that he'd slung over the back wall to air in the morning sun.

But Seimon's hard words began to echo around him and Eurig wondered how long it would be before they'd be able to talk it all through, without tantrums and abuse. Damn the golden haired boy for reminding him so vividly of Seimon! Had it been Hefin who'd responded with such hostility, Eurig would have been less surprised and perhaps not even cared too much; after all, Hefin had always been a bit of a Mammy's boy and taken Fflur's side in everything. But no... Hefin had shown an understanding of the human condition's curiously fickle nature that seemed beyond his fifteen years. Fflur had suggested that perhaps Seimon's disappointment was the greater because he and Eurig had been so close – and that his feeling of betrayal, therefore, was that much deeper. In that sense, Eurig could see how Seimon had, perhaps, lost considerably more than Hefin had, and that was why he needed to try to talk with him again.

After vehemently beating the dust of many months from the rug, releasing within its cloud some of the upset and frustration that had built up in the days since the row with his head-strong seventeen year-old, Eurig rolled it back over the living room floor and moved the table and dining chairs back to their place. He took in the new layout and was pleased. Now that 'The Warren' was no longer just for the odd weekend and summer holidays he needed to put his own stamp on the cottage. After much hassle he'd had the phone connected, and in time he'd replace the eccentric remnants that had accumulated over the year: curtains no longer matching changes of wallpaper in the family home and chairs too dated or loose-springed for everyday comfort. Eurig knew that when he came to chop them into sticks for the stove, each piece of furniture would surrender its bittersweet memories.

Eurig

With the grandfather clock's choked mid-day chime, you consider the promise of the dunes and relish the afternoon's possibilities. You strip. Rubbing the factor twenty sun block into your thighs and up into your groin, you become aroused at the prospect of meeting Dylan again. Catching sight of yourself in the cracked mirror of the wardrobe door you wonder whether to smear your pidyn *with sunscreen; you certainly don't want to get burnt there. You lick your forearm, already covered with sun lotion; it tastes unpleasantly chemical. You'll just have to risk sunburn if you take off your trunks!*

They'd met the previous afternoon. After an unsuccessful hour cruising a twenty-something, muscle-bound god with a conch-shell tattoo where others might have an appendix scar, Eurig had given up the chase. Lying on his towel in a shallow hollow, his head cupped in his hands, he mused on what might have been. Dylan, attracted by the genial look of an older man, sat on a low dune, partly concealed by a tussock of marram grass, and watched Eurig for a good ten minutes; he took in the leanness of his body, the greying at his temples and the black thickets in his armpits and groin. He feasted on the fantasy of their bodies coming together... but the pips from his watch broke through the reverie and signalled that his time in the dunes was up for another day. Eurig smiled at the man whose watch alarm had drawn his attention, and though he was unable to make out his features in the bright sunlight, he beckoned him over. They shook hands rather formally, Eurig thought, given that so many in the dunes were considerably more intimate on an altogether anonymous basis. They introduced one another, and as Dylan explained that he had to get back to the hospital for an evening clinic, Eurig lost his head in the boy's searching gaze.

Eurig

Still captured in the virid depths of Dylan's eyes, you lie back into the warm, soft sand beneath your towel and enjoy the random collision of thoughts. His tanned skin inviting your touch... the affectionate smile that drew you in... the unfashionably long hair, bleached by the sun and the sea's saltiness. And from the Mabinogi tales of your childhood comes the fabled Dylan Ail Môr, and Dylan becomes your child of the sea, within whose beauty you swim – until the shadow cast by a stranger dims your visions. The conch-shell tattooed boy stands over you, offering himself. Recognising that Dylan has stirred your emotions, you send the boy, by now quite confused and disappointed, on his way – and you dive back deeply into Dylan's sea.

Dylan

Showering quickly before changing into your uniform, you try to resist the lure of a sexual fantasy with the man in the dunes. He said his name was Eurig. An unusual name, but hardly a golden boy... but that's all right; you like the greying, older, slightly tarnished look. You doubt that he's much more than forty and ten years isn't such a gap. Perhaps his heart's golden? He seemed so mannerly, shaking hands and all; such courteousness is rare amongst the dune

89

cruisers. You try to conjure in your mind the friendly face attached to the body that has so turned you on, but the features are ethereal and quietly you concede that your mind is a bit one-tracked when it comes to the physical features of men. Yet it was something in Eurig's face that had deepened your interest. How tired his eyes looked, perhaps? Maybe there was some sadness in the face, too. Pulling on your trousers, you wonder if Eurig might not turn up the next day. The melancholy brought on by this doubt un-nerves you. You question the spell cast over you by Eurig's smile, which comes with transient vividness to your mind's eye.

Eurig

Passing through the gate by the buddleia bush, you consider the possibility that Dylan might stand you up; after all, you barely exchanged more than a dozen words. How was it possible that he'd aroused such a cauldron of feelings? How could you have been so stupid, so adolescent even, to have been seduced by those green eyes and allowed yourself to believe that he might actually fancy you? You push off the bleakness of the disappointment you foresee descending, should Dylan decide to stay away. You seek, instead, to occupy yourself in a search for the spear-leaved orache and viper's-bugloss that grow along the path amongst the thrift.

Dylan

You try to ignore the fact that you're being cruised and hope that the man who circles the rim of the hollow will leave you alone. The last thing you want, if Eurig does turn up, is for him to think you're copping off with someone else. When the gym-sculptured parody finally comes down into the hollow and struts his stuff, you recognise the boy with the conch-shell tattoo. With a smile, you ask if the antibiotics you'd prescribed him at the clinic the previous week have done their job and whether the crab lice you'd found in his groin

*and armpits are still driving him crazy at night. You don't catch the
boy's reply as he runs off over the brow of the hollow.*

Eurig

*You wonder only fleetingly why the cupid with the conch-shell
seemed so flustered as he pushed past you along the path where the
marram grass seemed especially spiky on the back of your legs.
Catching sight of Dylan in the hollow, sitting on a bleached tree-
trunk worn smooth by un-logged voyages in the Irish Sea, your
mind races. Might yesterday's mirage be exposed in the glare of a
new day's sun as no more than a brazen dune bum, randy for
anonymous intimacy? Do your baggy shorts betray the sexual desire
that quickens your breathing? Will you still find yourself in love, or
be stung by your crass stupidity?*

Dylan

*The relief that you feel, once you're alone again in the hollow, gives
a clue to the extent of your surrender. Under the spell cast by the
fleeting smile of the stranger for whom you now wait, you've dared
to think again about love after a broken love. What must you have
read into that smile in the hours since your meeting that has so
besotted you? Are you making a complete fool of yourself? But when
Eurig greets you with the most chaste of kisses on the cheek, you know
these are the wrong questions.*

They talked as they walked along the beach towards the island where
Llanddwyn's chaste isolation was held hostage by the low tide.
Neither noticed the nude bathers that marked the transition from
the gayer end nearer the point, nor the cute daddies – with their
bikinied women and sunburnt children to protect them – who
tended not to stray much beyond the forest boundary in the middle
of Llanddwyn Bay. Immersed in one another's intimacy, Eurig and

Dylan revealed the bits of their lives they hoped the other would find relevant and engaging. Bound by the charmed circles that each had cast around the other, both dared to believe they'd discover the meeting points that might hold them together and give a context to the carnality each now knew they would share.

Sitting on lichen covered stones that might once have been part of Dwynwen's convent on the island, Eurig told Dylan how, in the fifth century, King Brychan's daughter suffered for love and had then, much later, become the patron saint of Welsh lovers. With a cheeky smile, Dylan said that they'd better steer clear of syrupy drinks in case their hearts turned cold like Dwynwen's, or worse still, they both turned into ice like Maelon, her lover. Then Eurig led Dylan to Dwynwen's well, where legend had it that the fate of lovers could be determined in the movements of the fish that swam there. Dylan laughed when he saw the shallow, miry puddle and with an exaggerated sigh at the prospect of doomed fortune he said that the fish obviously didn't dance for the likes of them. Eurig waved his hands over the murky pit like a crazed, camp old witch, calling on the fish to reveal their secrets. Bending low over Dwynwen's well he caught the glint of something brilliant in the mud.

From the rock that had split so the dying Dwynwen could recline and bask in her last sunset, Dylan and Eurig watched the sky turn red and they thought up fables about the gold gimmal ring. The mud had come away easily enough from the ring's interlocking hands, and the heart that the fingers embraced had retained its lustre. Lost or thrown aside? Some careless lapse or the vengeful and deliberate action of an angry lover? Or perhaps the fish were telling them something after all? Then Dylan kissed Eurig deeply. Their senses sated with sensual pleasures and sex almost took them over. Eurig drew away, fearing that this exquisite promise might be washed away by grief and loss.

The tide rolled in over Malltraeth Bay's wide sands and the waves restored to Dwynwen a fragile virginity. The sun set, and they sat in silence, high up on the deserted beach, both hoping for a new beginning and wondering if they dared entrust it to the other. And when sex's possibility made their talking futile, they swam, confident that the effort would tire them and the cold numb their mutual desire. Later, wrapped in one another's tired arms at the sea's edge, where dying waves lapped their vulnerability, Eurig yielded to the whispered promise and the rhythm of Dylan's body.

Dylan

The familiar path in the firebreak through the Corsican pines, which down the years has always seemed endless, brings you all too quickly to the clearing where you've left your car. You want to accept Eurig's invitation to rest for the few hours that remain of the night, but you recognise that the odds are against there being much calm between you. You need at least a few hours sleep if you're to make it through the morning clinic. And you want some time by yourself to question your motives and consider the fishes' prophecy.

Eurig

Already missing Dylan, you lay on the chaise-longue and stare at the red light on the new answering machine, almost as though to de-code its Morse-like flashes. You are half afraid to listen to whatever voice has been recorded, in case its message pulls you back into the debris of your broken family. Eventually you hear Seimon say that he's sorry; he asks if you can meet. Through Fflur's window, the dawn bloodies the sky over Snowdonia. You tug the chaise across the living room, dragging the rug with it. Lying in its familiar embrace, grateful that you no longer have to watch the comings and goings of the men along the path just beyond the buddleia bush, you

roll Dwynwen's gimmal ring in your fingers. When Dylan comes
to you, you slip it onto his little finger and swim with him in the
dawn.

A Particular Passion

Over lunch, which they ate in the spring sunshine outside the Education Authority training centre, Ben Pasgen and his two colleagues wondered if either of the workshop facilitators had ever stood in front of a class of fourteen-year-olds; the theories they expounded seemed so untouched by practice.

'It's all very well saying we should question our motives for being involved in sex education,' Gwern said. A newly qualified teacher in his first job, his speech was instantly recognisable as Cardiganshire Welsh. He continued, 'I was just told that it was a part of the tutorial class-work and that I might get to go on a course if there's some spare cash at the end of the year. I don't have a motive for my involvement: I just feel coerced.' Catrin, the head of RE from the largest school in the area, said that since the Assembly's new Sex Education guidelines had come in they'd had to involve reluctant teachers who'd had no specialised training too, but at least their school policy was quite clear about what could and could not be taught; 'Our biggest problem as a group of staff,' she explained, 'is dealing with personal questions and disclosures. I know that kids can play up and they often just ask things to test you, or see if they can embarrass you, but sometimes you get the sense that a question is genuine. Just recently some of the girls in Year Eleven asked if I'd had sex before I was married.'

'What did you say?' Ben quizzed.

'I asked them why they wanted to know,' Catrin said straightforwardly. 'It's a good tactic with personal questions, it gives you a bit of time to think and it helps you judge if they're trying it on.'

'And what did they say?' asked Gwern.

'Well, one of the girls said she was feeling pressured by her boyfriend and another, who'd thought she was ready, had carted her boyfriend off to see the Family Planning people and they'd both come away feeling a bit unsure. They were talking so sensibly, and they wanted to know how I'd dealt with my first sexual experiences.'

'So how much of yourself do you give away, Catrin?' Ben asked, searching her face with his grey eyes.

'That's a hard one,' she said with a shrug. 'It all depends on what sort of life you've led, I suppose. I've only ever slept with one man and we did sleep together before we were married, but I was twenty-two and engaged and we kept having to put the wedding off because Paul's mother had cancer. I didn't mind sharing that with the girls... but perhaps if I'd had sex with two or three boyfriends when I was in college, or if I'd had an abortion at 15, or maybe if I was a lesbian, I might not have wanted to say too much. Kids can be bloody cruel if they think they've got something on you.'

Ben lay on the top bench, his head cradled in his hands; he felt the sweat trickle into his armpits. Except for the second Friday of the month, his slot on the duty rota of the gay line in Bangor, he spent every Friday evening at The Steamworks. The by-pass around Y Felinheli and the ludicrously fast A55 meant that he could get there from his remote hillside cottage in just over an hour. As the sauna's heat eased the tightness of the knots in his shoulders and soothed the pain of his rheumaticky hands, his preoccupation with the sex education workshop earlier that day, and Catrin's comments about answering personal questions, gave way to thoughts of sexual desire and gratification.

Some of the regulars were already there: Tony, the boy from 'parks and gardens', Gwyn and Iolo, the vicar and the GP who always came together, Eddy, who taught at the university in Bangor and Stan, the chip shop owner from Llandudno. Ben didn't knowingly have sex with any of this group, though in the steam room it wasn't always easy to know who was who; these were the men he sat around with and talked to about politics and travel, gardening and DIY. It was still early, but there were a couple of strangers that excited him; this was how Ben had grown to like it – anonymous sex was so uncomplicated. This way he could be certain, when he left The Steamworks, that no one would be likely to turn up on his door step or phone him at school... and he could be sure that he wouldn't become emotionally involved.

It wasn't that somewhere deep inside him he didn't yearn for one man to love and share his life with. A long time ago, nearly sixteen years, he'd made a choice to return to Gwynedd and immerse himself in Welsh life. Though Manchester had seemed tempting, since the gay scene had come into its own, offering freedoms and choices that would be out of reach in Meirionnydd, the chance to teach science in a new Welsh-medium school and to live his everyday life in his mother tongue touched him at his identity's core. He knew well enough that such a choice would demand that his gayness remain in the closet, but Ben Pasgen was neither disappointed nor dissatisfied with his life. Just like the peppered moth, the example he always cited to his GCSE class when explaining the theory of natural selection, he had adapted successfully to a potentially hostile environment.

Ben's experience of sex in The Steamworks was often bizarre, but it was always safe: it was as though the group voiced a silent message about self-preservation that no one transgressed. One of the staff replenished the supplies of condoms and lubricating gel once or twice through the course of an evening; like fruit or sweets, they lay in bowls on occasional tables for customers to help themselves. It was with some pride that Ben would occasionally reflect on the fact that for all his brief encounters, with perhaps fifty, seventy, even a hundred men a year, he'd never caught an infection. But then he wasn't complacent either, and knowing that some STIs developed no symptoms, he had himself checked over at the clinic in Wrexham every school holiday. Since the cute new consultant had arrived, Ben almost looked forward to these visits. His colleagues at school, the faithful few on the Parochial Church Council and the dwindling congregation at Eglwys Sant Pedr, his co-campaigners in Plaid Cymru and his friends in the choir would have been shocked and scandalised had they known of Ben's evenings at The Steamworks. Some, he felt sure, would be disgusted and want no more to do with him. Yet, he'd always been careful not to deliberately mislead people or lie to them, and in all the years he'd been back in Wales, no one had asked about his 'private life'. Perhaps the visible busyness of his days precluded, in most people's minds, any notion of him having a private life. But he knew well enough how people made assumptions about others… how they filled in the gaps of other people's lives with their own fancies and fictions. Ben couldn't know the untruths in which they'd clothed him.

For some weeks after the sex education workshop, when he was driving or in the middle of some renovation job on his cottage, Ben had thought about how he might respond if a student asked him about his sex life. He'd tried rehearsing different scenarios and anticipating responses, but gay and lesbian issues were not part of everyday conversation in the cafés of Dolgellau, the pubs of Trawsfynydd or the staff room at Ysgol Bro Meirion, so the imaginary role-play only led to an uneasy paranoia. He liked the idea of establishing a 'no personal questions' ground rule with his classes, but he also liked Catrin's suggestion: 'Ask them why they want to know'. He couldn't help wondering how many boys and girls, in his fifteen years at Bro Meirion, had been confused and tormented by the realisation that they were gay or lesbian and found no information or support at school. He remembered the fear and loneliness of his own school days. Ask them why they want to know, he repeated to himself.

When the question came it wasn't during a sex education lesson. This might have thrown Ben, had gay sex not surfaced again on all the front pages in connection with political sleaze and subconsciously prepared him. He'd encouraged the students in Wednesday's Year Ten tutor group to bring in cuttings from newspapers and magazines for comment and debate. Iddon, the brawny tight-head prop who secretly worried that he was the only virgin in the scrum, began the discussion.

'What about all these homos in Parliament, then?' he asked the class, holding up the front page of a tabloid with the headline *Queer Goings-on in the House*. A clutch of Iddon's gang began to giggle. Ben ignored them and addressed the class:

'Okay... this story's been running for a couple of days now. Has anyone else been following it?'

Manon put up her hand and said, 'That's the story I've brought in too, Sir...' and with a trace of scorn in her voice she continued, 'but my cutting is from *The Independent*.'

'Good, Manon,' Ben smiled. 'And anyone else? Hands up all of you who know something about this.'

Most of the class put up their hands.

'All right then,' Ben said, sitting on the table at the front of the class, 'why don't we ask Iddon and Manon to give a brief summary of how the two different newspapers have reported this story... and perhaps both of you would like to tell us what you think about it before we open up to the class. Okay? Iddon, why don't you start?'

'Sir, this story's about two MPs. They're both married men with kids,' Iddon lifted his right arm and dangled his wrist limply, 'but they've been having it off with other men.'

Some of his pack made cringing faces and grunting noises; signs of their disgust, Ben wondered, or just their own adolescent insecurity? Iddon continued, 'I think the main point in this article is that men like these shouldn't be trusted. They shouldn't be allowed to be MPs... and... well, Sir, I think they should all be put on an island and have their balls cut off.'

Iddon's supporters cheered and clapped.

'Thank you for that, Iddon,' Ben said, with a smile, anticipating the lively responses his proposed treatment for gay men might evoke. 'That's enough cheers or we'll have complaints from next door. Come on then, Manon, let's hear what you've got to say.'

She stood up and took a deep breath, as if trying to swell her tiny body to gain some authority: 'The main argument of this article,' she said with all the confidence of a regular eisteddfod winner in recitation and public speaking, 'is that for as long as our society remains intolerant of homosexuals and lesbians, and is reluctant to see them taking prominent positions in our public life, there will be men and women who will feel forced to lead double lives, a public life which seems to conform to society's expectations and a private life which is secret and furtive. And of course, if people feel they've got something to conceal, then they will hide behind lies and deception and so their integrity is called into question.' She looked around the class and wondered if her points had been put clearly enough. 'Personally,' she pushed a strand of hair back behind her ear, 'I feel very sorry for these two Members of Parliament, not because I approve of the way they've treated their families or misled their constituents, but because they have not felt able to be themselves. I'm sorry for them because they've had to live a lie and I would hope that our generation,' she paused and looked at Iddon and his supporters, 'I would hope that our generation will work to eliminate discrimination against homosexuals and be open to understanding their lifestyle. I see no reason, in the future, why we shouldn't have a lesbian leader of Plaid Cymru or why there shouldn't be a gay night at the Deri Arms in *Pobol y Cwm*. I don't understand why people are frightened and threatened by homosexuals, but I think the key to lifting the threat and easing the fear is better education.'

In the silence that gripped the class, Manon sat down triumphantly; even Iddon seemed to be held in the transient embrace of her challenge.

The class debate was slow to kindle. Iddon's ideas seemed too extreme for the majority, and were, anyway, quite impractical. Which island would they choose and wouldn't homosexuals hide if they knew they were going to be castrated? But Manon was accused of being too liberal; she hadn't considered the immorality of homosexuality or the corrupting influence people like that had on young people and on family life. And then Richard, one of Iddon's rugby mates, asked, 'Do you know any queers then, Sir?'

'Yes, a few,' Ben replied.

Iddon, rocking on his chair, asked cockily, 'You one then, Sir?'

'That's a very personal question, Iddon,' Ben responded with no trace of hesitation. 'Why would you want to know?'

'So that I can keep my back to the wall, Sir,' Iddon fired straight back.

His cronies laughed. Ben felt sick inside, but his face remained calm and in the second he gave to his thoughts, Miriam came back at Iddon, 'And what makes you think that Sir would even fancy you?'

The class's laughter cut her off and Iddon turned redder than a Comic Relief plastic nose.

'Well, thank you Miriam,' Ben said, trying to lighten the heaviness that pressed on him. 'You credit me with more taste than that, then?'

'Oh – he makes me sick, Sir,' Miriam said mockingly. 'He thinks he's sex on a stick.'

'That's enough, Miriam,' Ben said. 'I think Iddon is embarrassed enough, don't make it worse for him.'

'Yeah – well, Sir...' Miriam smiled at Ben. She liked him.

Tracy, one of the brassiest girls in the class, called from across the room, 'If you were gay then, Sir, who would you fancy?'

'Why would you want to know if I'm gay, Tracy?'

'Well,' she shrugged, 'then we could talk about men, Sir, you know, compare notes. What do you think about Robson Green or that gorgeous Michael Owen?'

'No, Tracy,' Ben said, shaking his head and smiling broadly. 'I don't think I'll be joining you in the girls' toilet to do make-up and talk about boys.' And addressing the class through their laughter, he continued, 'All right, let's try and pull the threads of this debate together and see what we're left with.'

After Ben had summarised their discussion and highlighted some of the sticking points he felt they ought to think about, Manon put her hand up: 'Mr Pasgen, you also left us with a question. You asked us why we would want to know if you are gay? You haven't actually said that you are gay... but you haven't said that you're not either.' She seemed to be judging essence and detail as she spoke. 'I think that the uncertainty you've left us with would be a really good thing for us to consider. I mean, if you, or any of our teachers at Bro Meirion are gay, does it make any difference to us in this class, to our parents, or to other kids and teachers in school?'

'Well done, Manon,' Ben said, his heart pounding so thunderously he wondered if those closest to him could hear it. 'I think that would be a good exercise to do during the week. It'll get us all thinking about our prejudices and our willingness – or unwillingness – to be tolerant and understanding. Good.... Thank you... all of you who contributed. We can come back to this discussion next week.'

The students erupted into exchanges around the room, which only the bell interrupted. As Ben dismissed the class the knotted muscles that had cramped his stomach and constricted his shoulders began to slacken and the rhythm of his heart regained its imperceptible certainty.

Miss Edwards the school secretary came to the junior science laboratory towards the end of the afternoon while Ben was teaching. She handed him a note from Mr Hopcyn, the headteacher: he needed to see Ben immediately after the bell. Ifan Hopcyn's straight-talking brusqueness had upset a number of the staff in the two years he'd been at Bro Meirion, but Ben could only speak as he found, and he liked him. As the children cleared away their things, Ben wondered if the Head had finally got a decision for him on the Year Twelve field trip.

Ben heard Catrin's advice echo in his mind and without flinching he looked into Ifan Hopcyn's grey eyes and asked, 'Why do you want to know if I'm a homosexual?'

'I've got the reputation of a school to defend and over three hundred adolescent boys to protect,' he said, almost pleading. 'Don't you think that those are good enough reasons for me to know?'

'But I'm not clear why the school's reputation needs to be defended nor what the boys need protecting from,' Ben replied firmly.

'I've heard that you told your Year Ten tutor group you might be a homosexual.'

'No,' Ben interrupted. 'We had a discussion about homosexuality which Iddon Jones and your daughter, Manon, introduced with clippings from today's newspapers.'

Ben recounted the direction of the arguments and explained how, when asked if he was gay, he'd deliberately chosen to be ambiguous so that the class would think about the issue in general terms and not get caught up in personalities.

'But I still need to know, Ben,' Ifan Hopcyn said. 'When parents start phoning me up worried about their children's physical and moral welfare I have to be able to put their minds at rest either by telling them that you're not a homosexual, or if you are, that I've taken all the necessary steps...'

'What are you talking about, Mr Hopcyn?' Ben asked, with an edge of disbelief in his tone. 'We're at the end of the twentieth century now... not the nineteenth!'

'People in this community will not tolerate a homosexual teaching their children, damn it!' Ifan Hopcyn banged his desk with a solid fist. 'We're not living in a left-wing London borough, Ben – this is *cefn gwlad* for God's sake,' he said, his voice raised.

A terse silence overwhelmed them.

When Ifan Hopcyn spoke again he'd regained his composure, 'I won't have homosexuals teaching at this school and I believe that the governors will support me in this.'

'You're going to put every teacher at Bro Meirion through this then,' Ben said. 'Some kind of purge, to cull the so-called morally unacceptable?'

'Is that your admission?' he asked.

Ben shook his head and smiling wryly he said, 'No... no, it's not an admission of anything. My answer to your question about whether I'm gay is the same as I gave to Year Ten this morning.'

'I'm sorry that you've chosen to be so unco-operative and unprofessional, Ben,' he said, strumming his fingers on his desk. 'I'll talk with as many of the governors as I can this afternoon and this evening; don't be surprised if you're suspended until I can call a full meeting of the board.'

Ben sighed and shook his head in utter disbelief. As he got up to leave he said quietly and with as much dignity as he could grasp, 'If your bigotry, Ifan Hopcyn, extends to the board of governors, then my days at Bro Meirion are surely numbered, so let me say this. I've given fifteen years of my working life to build the academic reputation of the science department in this school, and I've worked pretty damn hard to turn out some decent, well-rounded young people. Consider me unco-operative if you will, but don't ever call my professionalism as a teacher into question. If I am a gay man then think about this. Being gay wouldn't be something that got switched on like a light this morning. Fifteen years suggest that it is not my suitability as a teacher that's at issue here. Something far bigger is at stake.'

'Child protection is what's at issue here, Ben,' Ifan Hopcyn spat out. 'Like every parent of a child in this school, I'm concerned that no vulnerable boys are buggered by a sodomite.'

Ben was silenced by the affront of the Head Teacher's allusion. Closing the door of the office behind him a pain in the palm of his right hand made him wince.

Ben keyed into the memory of the CD player the track numbers of the opera's overture and Rienzi's aria from the beginning of act five. They played alternately at full volume, for there were no neighbours on Ben's hillside to be disturbed. He watched the colours of the sunset play on the river far below and the menacing clouds swirl around the giant's throne high across the valley. Wagner's music invaded the remotest recesses of Ben's consciousness, its turbulence routing the recollected insults, its tenderness pacifying his spirit.

The red flashes of the answering machine bore witness to the calls that the music had muted. Ben listened first to Gomer Prys, choir leader and governor at Bro Meirion: '...given your trouble it would be better if you don't sing at the Easter concerts.' Then Ieuan from the local Plaid campaign team, also on the governing board: 'Hopcyn's got it all wrong of course; I have told him, Ben. The stupid bugger thinks all gays are paedophiles... but then, you know, perhaps a lot of the locals will think that too... so, maybe, with this hanging over you, like, it won't do the election campaign any good to have you out canvassing. Sorry Ben.' And Ifan Hopcyn: '...I've talked with seven of the governors and the unanimous feeling was that we call an emergency meeting next week. Until then you're suspended. Do not come to school until further notice. I'll put all this in writing for you.' The same stabbing pain that had earlier caused his right hand to clench now contorted the left one.

In the minutes before the morning assembly, Manon, who'd heard enough from her father's study to know what was going on, persuaded four of her friends that it was the right thing to do. They had to stand against bigotry and injustice. When everyone else sat down after singing the hymn, the five remained standing. Manon, in her clearest eisteddfod voice, announced that she thought she might be a lesbian and wondered when she could expect to be suspended like Mr Pasgen. None of her four friends let her down, each voice rising above the commotion that was breaking out in the school hall:

'I think I'm a lesbian too....'

'I think I may be gay....'

Ifan Hopcyn called for silence and for a moment the hall became quiet. Then, to Manon's surprise, Tracy stood up in the row before them:

'It doesn't matter if Mr Pasgen is gay, he's the best teacher we've got,' she said, her voice faltering, betraying a softer, more vulnerable quality that surprised many in the assembly. And a cheer grew louder through the hall and more students rose to their feet. Mr Hopcyn's face went from red to purple. Though he called out for order, more than a third of the gathered students stood in defiance of his authority.

Ben knew nothing of the minor insurrection unfolding at Bro Meirion that Thursday morning; nor did he know that by the final bell of the afternoon, Manon and Tracy's unlikely alliance had given birth to a petition in his support, which had been signed by over four hundred of the school's six hundred pupils. Ben had thought he would spend the morning on the phone getting some advice from the teaching unions, but the morning sunshine was warm, so he sat in his garden and watched the insects dip into the blood red of the tulips cascading over the steep terraces. He rubbed balm into his palms and knuckles but the pain gnawed deeply. Through the open windows, resounding across the valley to the majestic Cader where Ben sometimes imagined God to be seated, Wagner's music soared and Rienzi's plea, *Almighty Father, look down upon me...* echoed Ben's own prayer. A prayer from another hillside in another time.

The Wedding Invitation

Just after the Penyffordd by-pass, Seth always begins to feel that Wales really is his home. He'll never belong in Liverpool even though the city has, for more than a decade, breathed into him the courage to become himself. As the dual carriageways of the Wirral and Deeside yield to the country roads that snake through the Clwydian range, the hills, with their lush, deep purples and greens of late spring, embrace Seth in a welcome home. Freddy Mercury's lament, The Great Pretender, bawling from the speakers on auto-repeat since driving into the Mersey Tunnel, jars with the mood of belonging that grips him. Ejecting Freddy, he pushes Leah Owen into the gaping mouth of the cassette player, the tape that had made him so homesick during that year in Israel with Jude.

Bala, for as long as he can remember, is the place where the journey from Liverpool to home has always been broken: for a pee, for chips, to buy a loaf of bread from the bakery that Seth's father is almost willing to admit bakes finer bread than he himself bakes in the Williams Family Bakery. In honour of this tradition Seth stops for ten minutes. He walks up the High Street as far as the Welsh Craft Shop to look at the Welsh wool sweaters rich in blues, reds and greens... and to finger the smoothness of a love spoon, before returning to the car and continuing the journey.

Passing the lake, just minutes west of Bala, Seth remembers a day spent walking in the hills around Llyn Tegid with the

Liverpool University Ramblers' Club. He hadn't known Jude well then, but they'd both talked a lot that day; mostly about Jude's interest in uncovering the story of a whole branch of his family that was gassed and burnt in the ovens at Auschwitz. He'd been fascinated by Jude, but had found him frightening too. Three years older, he'd talked about how learning of the fate of his family in that Polish death camp had woken him up to the Nazi persecution of gays during the years of the Third Reich, and how this forgotten history had become the focus of his doctoral thesis. That had been in '86 or '87, before Seth had woken up to himself. His sense of identity then had lacked honesty or integrity, and he'd found such talk painful.

Jude hadn't been invited to Seth's sister Naomi's wedding. Seth cast his mind back to their breakfast, earlier that Friday morning.

'You can't disappoint your sister, Seth,' he'd urged. 'You can't just decide not to go.'

The arguments around why Jude was being excluded had been almost exhausted over the past weeks. Seth had hated being the messenger, especially when that had involved reminding Jude of his mother Ceinwen's particular animosity.

"A traditional family wedding in the countryside, at the Welsh heartland; that's no place for the two of you to be seen together," Seth had mimicked Ceinwen's rising pitch. "And it's not right anyway that a man should keep such close company with another man! People in the village will talk! Not to mention that this other man is a Jew..." They'd both been able to laugh at Ceinwen's histrionics. 'But then she always backtracks too,' Seth went on, 'pretending she's got your interests at heart and worrying that you'd feel left out with everyone speaking Welsh!'

'That's a joke!' Jude had exploded. 'Has she forgotten that Chris – the groom, for God's sake – is a Bristol man who talks like he's got Victoria plums in his mouth?'

But their roles had been cast, and over their coffee that morning the hurt, but understanding lover had persuaded Seth that he should attend the wedding alone.

The recollection of Jude speaking his pain that morning reopens the wound of Seth's parents' denial and rejection. It smarts deeply, triggering a yearning to hold Jude, and be held by him. He pulls over into a lay-by at the side of the lake, and at the water's edge wills the beauty of the afternoon to calm the emotional cross-currents coursing through him: love for Jude pulling against the loyalty he believes is owed to sister and parents. For seven years and three months he's shared a love with Jude that neither of them had ever believed might be possible. Since they've known about them as a couple, Seth's parents have denied the reality of his happiness with Jude. Ceinwen, from the beginning, has only ever referred to him as that Jewish man. As the storm rages, Seth wishes that his parents could take a leaf from Jude's mother and father.

The Canters hadn't actually welcomed Seth with open arms either; they too had found it hard to accept that their son loved another man. But, with time, they'd softened: Nina Canter had even bought Seth a boxed set of Edith Piaf CDs one birthday after hearing that Piaf's passion moved him to tears.

Back in the car, fingering the steering wheel in hesitation, Seth pictures the uproar that the phone call he wants to make will create: *Dwi'n aros yn Lerpwl efo Jude....* He imagines how Ceinwen, on hearing his refusal, will be even more hostile towards Jude. She'll go on about how he can't show greater loyalty to that Jew than to his own family: 'You have to come to the wedding... you can't stay in Liverpool – not this weekend.'

And he pictures Jude, more dear to him than anyone in the world, and remembers how reasonable he's been through the whole messy affair.

With Piaf at full volume Seth continues west. After Dolgellau he winds the car with the Mawddach to the wide estuary and the coast. The village signpost still bears the scars of the fatal accident more than a year ago, one of its poles rusted and bent, the bold lettering pitched at sixty degrees. Not much seems to have changed in the village. Before reaching the house he passes the bakery: the sign, *M. Z. Williams & Son – Fine Bakers... Baking your Daily Bread since 1922* has been repainted. Miss Morris, who's worked for his father for half a lifetime, is standing at the door talking to Mrs Caradog the Minister's wife... about their rig-outs for the wedding, most likely. Mrs Caradog will be exasperated, as is her way, by the prices of everything in Chester... she always shops in Chester, Browns, so dependable! Miss Morris will be retelling, in every detail, how Nancy Parry helped her choose from the lovely selection of twin sets in stock at London House... new for the spring and very reasonable. Miss Morris recognises Seth and waves a welcome, which he returns. At the village's only traffic light he turns right into Enlli View Road. The Llŷn Peninsula and Bardsey Island fill the windscreen after the turn. The signpost still shows stains from a dousing with green paint. The Language Campaign seems years ago now.

By dinnertime that evening Ceinwen Williams had re-ironed her son's shirt, sponged and pressed his suit and expressed her distaste for the tie he'd chosen to wear. Seth cares little for his mother's taste in ties and is actually grateful that she'd troubled with his suit... but Jude had ironed his shirt that morning and her re-ironing of it was an interference that he resents. He hadn't expected to be alone with his mother. Naomi had been home most of the week and he'd assumed that she would be about, fussing. But Seth had caught only the briefest glimpse of his sister. Her best friend from school and now her bridesmaid-to-be, Shân, had phoned as Seth had walked in through the door to say that her car had broken down the other side of Dinas Mawddwy. Naomi had rushed to rescue Shân, while Chris was checking that his family were all settled at the George III Hotel in Penmaen Pool.

Stirring the gravy, just Seth and his mother in the kitchen, he ventures to share his most recent good news: that from September Jude will be Senior Lecturer in Modern History at Liverpool University. Ceinwen straightens her back as she lays the masher on the worktop beside the steaming pan of mashed potato. She spits the words out in her precise Caernarfonshire Welsh: 'That Jewish man's success is none of my concern. It's time you settled down... properly! Family weddings are not the time to bring disgrace on us.'

Still stirring the gravy, and not looking at her, Seth talks about how much he loves Jude; how it's a creative and whole and special and wonderful relationship... and that they're both very happy together. Surely that's what's important... to have found happiness and not be a lonely, twisted, insecure, frightened person? But before all the words are spoken, Chris and Naomi burst into the kitchen. Ceinwen's eyes catch Seth's for a fleeting second, pleading – and demanding at the same time – that no more be said.

The family gathers around the table to eat. Ceinwen had decided it would be convenient to all concerned that the five of them should eat at home, and then go over to the George III after Chris's family had rested and eaten. Seth is struck by the strangeness of English conversation around the dining table of his family home. His mother speaks English with an affected twang. His father's grasp of the language is laboured and makes him sound a bit stupid, which he isn't. Naomi's Welsh accent, however, is scarcely audible.

The wedding talk gives way to disconnected snippets from work, respective family histories, last year's holidays, the new ovens in the bakery and the price of Welsh lamb, which Ceinwen believes to be robbery, but then Welsh is so much tastier than New Zealand! And then Chris asks Seth how Jude is.

Seth smiles at him and fleetingly wonders whether his question is born of naivety or rebellion. He shares the news of Jude's success in getting the Senior Lectureship.

'Well done, Jude!' murmurs Chris, adding, 'It's a shame he can't be with you this time.'

Seth's father Mostyn stops eating, his fork poised, his eyes fixed on the remains of the Welsh lamb's leg. Ceinwen has flushed, her face as crimson as her frock, her stare intent on silencing Chris. He seems oblivious, confident even that he'll be his own man, son-in-law to the imperious Ceinwen or no.

'Has Jude's thesis been published yet?' he asks. Ceinwen's rudeness reveals how flagrant she finds Chris's disregard for her version of the family code. Addressing Naomi directly in Welsh she snaps, 'Chris must understand that Seth's misadventure with that Jewish man is not acceptable family conversation.'

'If you want to say something to Chris,' Naomi answers in English, 'you'd better speak to him in a language that he can understand!'

Mostyn lays his fork on his plate, and takes Ceinwen's shaking hand on the table.

'Our background and generation,' he murmurs to Chris with profound humility, 'make it difficult to accept Seth's choices in life. We would rather you spared us the embarrassment.'

The dining room falls silent but as the seconds slip away the chink of knives and forks fills the quiet that had separated the family.

Chris is offered more lamb, which he declines. Ceinwen's

interpretation of his refusal is explained to the gathering... that he's saving room for her *tarten 'fale*. On some previous visit Chris had raved about Ceinwen's apple tart, which had thrilled her no end and scored him lots of points, and he'd eaten three huge slices at a single sitting. On every subsequent visit Chris had been served Ceinwen's *tarten 'fale* for dessert. As she rises from the table she turns to Naomi requesting her help in the kitchen.

As though Seth were invisible, Mostyn says to Chris, almost by way of apology, 'Ceinwen really can't cope at all with Seth being one of the sons of Sodom.'

Chris, moving closer to Seth and putting his arm around his shoulder, shakes his head and replies, 'To deny Jude's existence is sad. As Seth's brother-in-law I'll respect his integrity. I won't become part of your denial, Mostyn!'

Mostyn's face softens and, nodding his head slowly, he answers, 'Perhaps that's how it should be in these modern times. Ceinwen and I haven't experienced city life; in our *milltir sgwâr...*' Breaking off, he searches for the English idiom and then, with a prompt from Seth continues, 'In our square mile of life such a thing is sinful and unnatural, bringing diseases and disgrace.' Silence falls over the table again.

Seth feels like hugging them both for their honesty but is prevented by uncertainty from even speaking. His father's pain is so real, and as much as he wants to acknowledge it, Seth doesn't want him to think that he accepts even a hair's breadth of his position. Chris, in a gesture that further emphasises his support for Seth, draws him closer until their heads touch and, almost in a private whisper, asks, 'When are you and Jude coming to visit us in Bristol?'

For a moment, before Seth mouths the words accepting Chris' invitation, he sees the agony tearing through his father's face and he knows that he'll never come home again.

As Seth and Chris begin to talk about the things they might all do in Bristol, Mostyn excuses himself, explaining that he needs to check that everything is ready for later that evening when, alone in the bakery, he'll bake bread for the village through the night. 'But I'll need help with the apple tart,' Chris jokingly protests.

Mostyn forces a laugh and leaves them.

'I really appreciate you standing with me, Chris,' Seth thanks him.

After eating too much apple tart, Seth and Chris offer to wash up the dinner dishes, so the two women disappear to make themselves ready for the get-together at the pub. Mostyn turns up in the kitchen, dressed and ready to go, just in time to put the dried dishes away.

The spring breeze blowing up the Mawddach from Cardigan Bay, seven miles away, has soured the promise of a mild evening. The George III at Penmaen Pool on the estuary echoes with Bristolian accents, all the rooms having been booked by Chris' family and friends months in advance. After ten minutes Seth begins to feel out of place. These are Chris and Naomi's family, not mine, he thinks. With a deepening anxiety about his need to censor whatever he might say, in case he causes some upset, Seth begins to wish he'd stayed home in the village. Regretting that he hadn't come in his own car he begins to feel trapped. He looks into his pint of Guinness... out at the river... thinks about Jude... looks into his pint again. Then Chris breaks into Seth's longing to leave and introduces his best man, Robert.

Alone together at a window overlooking the toll bridge that crosses the river, Seth and Robert become instantly easy with one another. Seth can't work out why neither Chris nor his sister have ever mentioned Robert before.

'Call me Robby,' he says, and before long they've progressed to scoring the two barmen. 'I reckon they're both trade, what d'you think?'

'Maybe... I hadn't given it much thought,' Seth responds with a coy smile.

'You can have the one with curly hair,' Robby gestures with a wink. 'I've only scored him a seven on the bed-able scale. Now that dark rugby player type... he gets a nine in my book!'

Not being that interested in scoring with either of the barmen, Seth asks him, 'How do you know Chris and Naomi?' Robby's life history spans the next half hour and another pint of Guinness.

While Robby's taking a pee Seth realises that he's cheered up. The alcohol has eased the tension that had tied knots across his shoulders as the day wore on, and meeting Robby has made him feel less a stranger in his own land. He watches the cars as they drive parallel to the river's edge and turn to cross the toll bridge, their headlights catching the bats in flight. He loves this river and its valley; he knows every mile of it from cycle rides, walks and childhood explorations, from the wide estuary with its railway bridge at Barmouth to its trickling source in the wild hills of Meirionnydd above Coed y Brenin. He remembers expeditions to the Clogau and Gwynfynydd gold mines and the adventures.... Robby returns, all smiles: 'The bar man's name is something unpronounceable in Welsh – no vowels! He does play rugby and he lives in. We're meeting up later on. Wish me luck!'

Much later, Seth is sitting at the kitchen table with Naomi.

Sharing what's left of the *tarten 'fale*, and drinking cups of tea, she talks about the old friends she's met again that evening, while Seth listens. She talks about Chris' family and tries to make the family connections for him. Then Seth chats about Robby and she can't believe that he's got a date with the bar man.

'Are you happy?' Seth asks. She replies, nodding, *'Hapus iawn.'*

The kitchen door opens and Ceinwen joins them. Naomi reaches for a mug and pours her some tea.

'Are you all ready for tomorrow?' she asks Naomi, who nods. 'We're proud that you're marrying so well even though we were disappointed when you first announced the engagement,' Ceinwen ventured once again onto dangerous ground, 'marrying into an English family and all... I'll have to speak with my grandchildren in a foreign language.'

'*Paid a dechra Mam, nid heno,*' Naomi warns. 'Don't let's go over this again, it's all been said before, not tonight of all nights.'

Seth breaks in, asking his mother why she finds it so hard to accept that her children are making the choices that are right for them... and not for her... not for other people. Naomi bangs her mug on the table, '*Paid ti a dechra chwaith, Seth,*' she points with her finger, don't you start either!

Seth gets up from the table, kisses Naomi on the cheek and goes to leave the kitchen.

'*Oes gen ti un i dy fam hefyd?*' Ceinwen wants him to kiss her too.

He turns at the door: 'No I haven't got a kiss for you. I won't play by your rules any more. If it's your choice to deny me, and the people and relationships that are important to me... if it's your choice to be so rude as to call Jude *that Jewish man* all the time...' Seth is gathering steam now. 'If you can't accept me and my choices then it would be better if I didn't come home again. There... I've said it.' Seth closes the kitchen door behind him.

From the bedroom window Seth can see the lights of Barmouth across the wide estuary mouth where the waters of the Mawddach join the bay. In the far distance the shimmer of Pwllheli's lights seem to dance with the stars on the low horizon. He grew up with the view from this window. He knows its moods... wild at times, ever changing, always beautiful. Its

117

familiarity is a comfort to the finality of his words: *It will be better if I don't come home again.*

Beginning to undress, the thought strikes Seth that at this time of night he can be back home in Liverpool in just two hours. He thinks about the three pints of Guinness and then about Naomi. Having removed all his clothes, he slips naked between the fresh cotton sheets and tries to conjure the warmth and presence of Jude's body next to him. In Jude's arms, in the absolute knowledge and confidence of their love for one another, sleep comes easily.

Walking the few hundred yards to the chapel, Seth reflects on the rightness of his decision not to flee back to Liverpool in the small hours. Rising early, he had walked a couple of miles through the village and its immediate surroundings, along the beach and up into the centre of the ancient stone circle in Cae Cynhaeaf, the field behind the parish church, where he'd said goodbye to his home patch. Back at the house by eight thirty, little was said at the breakfast table, indeed, he'd been left with a pot of coffee and the local paper. Children from the village still gather at the chapel gates, just like he and Naomi had done when they were children. The kids distract him... bring him from his thoughts to face Robby, standing at the doors of the chapel with an usher, smiling mischievously as he climbs the steps.

Naomi looks beautiful. Seth is surprised that she must have won the battle against tradition, since she is walking down the aisle between her parents. Ceinwen looks elegant, but then this is the occasion on which she has to out-do Mrs Caradog the Minister's wife, who, in Seth's judgement has chosen the wrong colour. Miss Morris hasn't been let down by the new spring collection in London House. The Bristol set look city sophisticated, like a troupe of extras from the set of an American soap opera. Robby looks so stunningly handsome Seth gets an erection. Mr Caradog handles the bi-lingual service well; Naomi says her vows in Welsh, Chris speaks his in English. It's a simple, dignified ceremony, and most importantly, Mr Caradog keeps his Welsh orator's tongue from straying.

The village park is used for the photographs, rhododendrons providing a deep purple backdrop. Anti Ceridwen tells Seth loudly that it's time he took some lucky girl down the aisle. Anti Delyth joins in, 'Are you going steady yet?' The two sisters agree with one another that Seth would make some girl a good husband. They share their observations with anyone within earshot who can understand Welsh. Seth smiles at his aunts but beneath the smile are thoughts miles from their delusions. But he plays the family game, one last time.

The newly-weds drive off at about half past four, signalling the end of things. No evening bash. Naomi had been to too many weddings where everything seemed to drag into a drunken all-nighter. The reception had been fine, with good food and everyone on strict orders to keep speeches short. There'd been a lot of laughter. Robby had camped up a bit when he'd had the stage, but his contribution was polished and funny. He'd even learnt two sentences of Welsh, which were applauded wildly.

Back at the house Seth changes into jeans and a sweater and carries his few things out to the car. Mostyn joins him on the pavement in front of the house, 'Thanks for making the family whole on this special day.' He puts out his hand to be shaken.

Seth shakes his head; 'The family wasn't whole Dad, not when I've had to pretend to be someone that I'm not! How can the family have been whole when the person I live with and love is excluded because of yours and Mam's misguided sense of what was right?' Seth flushes, gulps 'Goodbye' and turns away.

Freddy Mercury's The Great Pretender is playing on auto-repeat along the Mawddach to Dolgellau and beyond. Passing through Bala without a stop, Piaf's *Non, je ne regrette rien* persuades Seth to leave whatever lingering doubts he harbours deep in the surrounding mountains. At Penyffordd, where the dual carriageway begins, Seth aches for Jude's touch of reassurance. He begins to welcome the freedom that Liverpool, just half an hour away, has helped him claim.

Jude isn't home. Alongside his note there's an envelope addressed to them both. The card inside announces: *Jude Canter and Seth Williams, Eli and Nina Canter request the pleasure of your company at the wedding of their daughter Louise, to Joshua Rosenberg.*

Eucharist

Kneeling at the communion rail, I wondered if it had been a free choice. In as much as any choice could be free, I supposed that it was so, but then people are always influenced by outside forces. Social norms, religious myths and beliefs, the political breezes of the age.... But yes, loving men in that way, and loving Joel in particular, finally hadn't felt right; out of tune, somehow, with the sacred music inside. The priest, Dafydd, was at the other end of the rail administering the Sacraments. I knew him professionally and we'd even met at a few social events, but our acquaintance wasn't a friendship that could share such secrets.

It had been twelve years since I'd last looked into Joel's open, wise face. We'd kissed and said goodbye again, for hadn't we been saying goodbye for weeks? In twelve hours the plane landed at Heathrow and I'd taken the train to my new home and a new job. We wrote, regularly to begin with, but the letters stuttered into infrequency as time passed. Joel's parish responsibilities had increased, while my own life also took on a crazed busyness as I embraced the challenge of ministering to six congregations.

Mrs Efans, a member at Bethania in the village, had been the post woman for forty years. '*Un o San Francisco heddiw Mr Llwyd*,' she'd say, handing me letters posted in the city that had been my home. Gwenda, as I was later invited to call her, had taken to knocking my door to hand-deliver in the first weeks after

121

I'd arrived. In her eyes, such regular contact with the new minister back from America gave her status in our isolated, closed community. She had noticed that I wore my shirts open at the chest, showing all my hair, that my coffee mugs declared jokey slogans and that I listened to rock music.

I spilled my coffee on reading that Joel was dead. His most recent letter, in July last year, had told of a move to Boston. A letter full of excitement and hope in new beginnings... new movies to look out for and recent productions at the San Francisco Opera. Nothing to suggest a slowing down. Not a hint of ill health. No tell-tale signs of being one of the thousands of worried well. The letter from Cheryl was unexpected and, once opened, unwelcome. She'd seen him in November, Kaposi's Sarcoma disfiguring his gentle face and the first signs of dementia cracking his intelligent, sometimes highbrow conversation. He'd died a few days before Easter. I wanted to cry. I wanted to hold Joel within that same strong tenderness we'd shared for nearly four years, to look into his face again and say, 'I love you.' A coffee stain edged further into the whiteness of the tablecloth.

I sought the sanctuary of routine, washing up the few dishes lying used by the sink. I placed the coffee stained tablecloth in a bucket of cold water. The gas bill was opened and processed for the next Presbytery meeting. I stripped my bed and loaded the washing machine. But as the possibility of routine's sanctuary gave way to despair, I sat in the window seat, with its view of Glan y Mawddach and Garn Gorllwyn across the wide estuary, and wept. With no more tears but a heaviness that was hard to shoulder, I walked up into the hills behind the village and sat searching into the waters of Cregennen. I wondered when Joel might have picked it up. Surely since the days of our intimacy? In all the years of celibacy I'd never considered the possibility that the virus might be harboured somewhere in the nucleus of a white blood cell. But now the possibility gnawed.

Walking along Ffordd Ddu, I yielded to God's embrace and lying in the sun I breathed in the rich smells of heather, bracken and sheep droppings. The Healer, who'd always tended the wounds of my lifetime's struggle with a sexuality that was generally despised and mistrusted, comforted and re-assured my troubled mind. The sun warmed my face, inviting my imagination to wander again with Joel in the California sun. The camping trips to Yosemite... the retreats at the house in Bodega Bay where we'd read Anne Sexton and Dylan Thomas aloud to one another to ease the mental fatigue brought on by heavier theological tomes, and where we'd made love in the hot tub on the deck under the stars. I remembered the pumpkin festival at Half Moon Bay; the garlic ice cream in Gilroy that had made Joel sick... and the peace of the Rose Garden in the Berkeley Hills, shattered by the Argentinian students' demonstration against the Malvinas war. And I wept again, but now the tears were less bitter. I had come to appreciate that what I'd shared with Joel had been a rich gift.

That spring evening, in the vestry of Bethania, only six gathered for the mid week prayer-cum-bible meeting – *y seiat*. We read Psalm One Hundred and Sixteen together. Some of it had come to me, mouthed over and over, during my mind's sojourn with Joel, and again as I climbed down from the hills to the village late in the afternoon. Words that had been the source of comfort and strength to troubled people for more than two thousand years, had also comforted me. Gwenda Efans took her neatly ironed handkerchief from the shambles of her handbag. Wiping away the silent tears she told how she'd recited the same Psalm, from memory, to her comatose husband in Bangor hospital.

Gwenda's words recalled for me the cavernous pits of grief into which she and many others in my congregations had descended over the years at times of loss. The fatal car accidents; the terminal cancers; the two cot deaths in one family; suicides and so many divorces. I'd walked alongside, and sometimes quite literally held up so many who'd experienced lost hope, uncertain faith and the wrenching hurts of separation. I realised that the news of Joel's death had sparked none of these within me.

The *seiat* ended with cups of tea, relaxed conversation and Dilys Morris-Jones the newsagent's bara brith. After we'd talked, drunk tea, and eaten; all the rituals done, people made their way home. After locking up the building, I walked back to the manse intending an early night.

Cheryl's letter lay open on the table. The sight of it brought Joel back to me. Sitting, watching the lights across the estuary play on the waters of the in-coming tide, I began to make some sense of my feelings. I was sad about Joel's death, but not grieving for him, for hadn't I already grieved the loss of our relationship at the time of my return to Wales? But I was shocked that Joel had been infected with HIV and that he'd developed AIDS. And I was anxious – even afraid, because our communion had been carnal at a time before safer sex and condoms had become routine.

I got the number of the National AIDS Helpline, dialled without hesitation, and spoke with the counsellor. I had to stifle my need to persuade her that Joel couldn't have been HIV positive all those years ago. Her voice was pacifying, but my anxiety only deepened when she said that she couldn't speculate as to when he'd been infected. She talked to me for a long time about testing. The implications of a positive or negative result, how the choice had to be informed, and that before deciding to be tested I'd need to have some fairly clear idea of what I'd do if the result were positive. She was patient and understanding; I could hardly take it all in. She gave me the phone number of a clinic at the hospital in Wrexham where the test could be done. It was past midnight when I hung up the phone.

My blood was drawn off and the small glass vial was sealed in a plastic bag marked BIOHAZARD in bold, red letters.

'It will be a week before the result comes back, Iwan,' the nurse said in broad Glaswegian. 'You do have to come back to get the result. We don't give HIV results by letter or over the phone.' The doctor had been careful, before taking the blood, to establish that it was legitimate to test me and she'd asked about risky behaviours... unprotected sexual intercourse... shared injecting equipment.

'Risky gay sex then,' she said as she wrote on the anonymous file.

The tears that blurred my vision and forced me into a lay-by on Llandegla Moors betrayed the first conscious realisation that I'd been hurt by the everyday language of the clinic: risky gay sex was an abridged version of all that I'd shared with Joel.

Routine carried me for seven days. The doctor was solemn when she confirmed the positive result of the blood test, and Ali, the Glaswegian nurse held my hand for some time; he was very tender. Somewhere, inside white blood cells, deep within the tissues of my body, there was a piece of biochemical grammar that had the potential to write a sentence in my genes, an instruction that would bring on cell death. The virus, coursing through my blood, waited for tomorrow. As it had done in Joel, tomorrow or some other tomorrow, it would cause my body's immune system to fail.

High above the village I made for the waters of Cregennen and the solitude that the mountains offered. I yearned for a quietness of mind, but a patchwork of thoughts had been woven in the hours since I'd been told, and my emotions lurched chaotically. Anxiety... confusion... joy... despair. The beauty and quiet of the mountain lake, shimmering in the early morning sunlight, were not infectious, and the thought looms continued to weave. I sought to grasp at the joy that my choice of celibacy now brought. The certainty that the virus, which lay dormant, had infected no one since my return from San Francisco.

'This is the Bread of Life,' Dafydd said, standing before me and placing the wafer on my out-stretched palm. It stuck to my tongue. Somewhere, in a distant cavern of my mind, I heard the echoes of my own prayers over the elements, on the one Sunday in the month that my tradition allowed. 'One Bread, One Body, One Lord of All, One Cup of blessing which we bless.' Anxiety and confusion gripped me as the wine dislodged the wafer from my tongue....

'This is the Blood of Christ.'

Joel came to me, offering comfort. I reached for the warmth of his touch. But the solace of his presence dissolved into the sorrowful words of Cheryl's letter, describing the cancer and dementia that had killed him. I swallowed, knowing that through my Communion, the Body of Christ would become infected. And with a pain that paralysed, the thought looms wove into the fabric of my being the first of many malignancies. Joel, too, had been blighted by my love.

Food For Thoughts

'A priest for God's sake!' Uwe's irritation was tinged by a heavier accent than usual. 'Why didn't you mention it before so we could have discussed it?' Vivid images from his years at a Catholic boarding school near Aachen flashed before him. The priests had drunk themselves celibate, then taken delight in spanking the naked bottoms of pubescent boys with a slipper, while railing against masturbation and the sins of the flesh. What had Tecwyn been thinking about? A litany of expletives competed with the chopping of an onion on the hardwood board. He always swore in his mother tongue; it was more expressive, coming from his guts. And besides, when he swore in English the silly-sounding words made him laugh. With one swipe of the knife across the chopping board he heaped the onions into the pan with the oil, garlic and chillies and through the hissing, muttered '*Arschloch.*' Tecwyn smiled and handed his lover a gin and tonic, then, with a tap on Uwe's bottom and a blown kiss, said, 'Some arse-holes are very nice!'

Uwe smiled sardonically: 'So who is this priest you've invited for dinner?'

Tecwyn described Nick the Vic, so dubbed by his group of early-bird swimmers. The black hair and brown eyes; the power of his breaststroke across the near deserted pool; his banter in the changing room, always too cheerful for that time of the morning; the Prince Albert that he sometimes tugged just to tease the ones who stared lustfully at him in the shower.

'So why did you invite him?' Uwe asked. 'Surely not because of his muscles, or is it some fascination for a forbidden piece of fruit with the ring through his *Schwanz*?'

Tecwyn steered the conversation into more serious waters, asking, 'Isn't the whole point of tonight that we hear as many views as possible; to help us decide?' He thought for a moment and elaborated, 'Since Nick is gay, he should understand our situation. Since he's a priest, maybe he can help us thrash out the heavy moral stuff?' With that he carried the tray of newly polished silverware into the dining room, leaving Uwe to start shelling the Dublin Bay prawns.

Uwe Greven, a consultant physician in genito-urinary medicine and pretty ace cook, had lived for six-going-on-seven years with Tecwyn ap Eifion who couldn't toss a salad unsupervised and was the only male family planning consultant working in Wales. They'd met at a Millennium Eve party, spent the first three days of the new century in bed together, and were an item by Valentine's Day. Both were out in every aspect of their lives. At work neither had felt it an issue, but then AIDS had brought lots of gay men into GUM. In Family Planning, being gay seemed to be a real advantage as it was non-threatening to the majority of women who'd traditionally cornered the field. At home, the house they'd bought and done up together bore all the hallmarks of fine taste, made affordable by considerable investment from their ample joint income. They loved their home, and loved to share its comforts with houseguests.

In their wider family life Uwe and Tecwyn realised their good fortune too. The Grevens, despite their Catholic piety, had demonstrated their acceptance of the situation with grace and showed genuine affection for Tecwyn through Christmas and birthday gifts. Tecwyn's mother, Arfona Lewis liked Uwe more than her two current sons-in-law, one of whom she found stupid, the other she considered pompous and English. She shared with him a love of opera, especially the Germans. In the four years since being widowed it was she, not Tecwyn, who accompanied Uwe to the Welsh National's two seasons at the Liverpool Empire and Opera North's at The Lowry. They'd even travelled to Bayreuth together for The Ring, leaving Tecwyn to tend his garden, feed her cats and work on the gay novel he was hoping to enter for one of the major prizes in the National Eisteddfod.

From the kitchen, Uwe asked, 'Nia is coming tonight, isn't she? Doesn't she study ethics or moral philosophy?'

'I think so,' Tecwyn replied, 'but she's been invited because Judith's a lawyer... we need some lesbian input.'

'So Mike and Tara are the token straights, then, are they?' Uwe surmised, totally unconvinced by the whole idea.

Coming back into the kitchen Tecwyn threw the tea towel he'd been using to wipe stray fingerprints from the silver at Uwe.

'Of course!' he exclaimed. 'And before you ask any more stupid questions, Richard and Penri are coming because they're the gay men we've been friends with longest. And Arfona is my mother!'

Cutting the pork fillets lengthways to make pockets that would later be stuffed with prunes and sultanas, Uwe asked, 'Has it ever struck you that our dinner guests might think we're being selfish? Perverse? What do we do if they're all against our idea?' It seemed to Uwe that to go ahead after soliciting their friends' opinions and meeting their disapproval would surely be worse than just doing it and letting them all find out later. Tecwyn answered, 'Why should any of them disapprove? Besides, the whole point isn't to ask anybody for permission!'

Tecwyn dug up the parsnips, leeks and carrots that Uwe wanted to roast in goose fat. He cut some young sprigs of rosemary, lifted two heads of garlic and pulled a bunch of parsley from the herb garden. All the time he kept wondering if Uwe was right; that really it was no one's business but their own. Since they'd virtually decided to go for it, they might just as well get on with it. Uwe would hit forty before Christmas and he'd be thirty-six in the spring; they couldn't leave it too long.

Arfona Lewis had unpacked her overnight bag and was already helping Uwe in the kitchen when Tecwyn came in with the herbs and vegetables. She kissed her son and addressing him in Welsh asked, 'How was your week? Have you any more of your manuscript for me to proofread?'

Tecwyn wondered what she'd make of the sexual encounter his main character had enjoyed with a man in a gay sauna. Tecwyn had become so sexually aroused writing it that he'd virtually dragged Uwe to the floor, where their own sex had been as greedy as anything he'd written into Iolo Pawl's adventures. Before Tecwyn could answer his mother, she'd taken the basket of vegetables, and was asking Uwe, 'Have you got a knife? How d'you want them cut?'

Sitting across the kitchen table, Tecwyn watched his mother as she peeled and chopped. He wondered whether to forewarn her about the sex scene before handing her the pages, but he found it difficult to talk to her about sex. He appreciated the absurdity of his reticence; didn't he spend all his working hours talking quite comfortably about condoms, pills and other useful things with the safety-conscious sexually active? Perhaps he didn't need to say anything. Hadn't she surprised and shocked the critics with her last novel? The only one of the five she'd written which dealt with anything explicitly sexual, it was the story of a fifty-something widow's aching need for the intimacy her husband's death had stolen from her. Tecwyn remembered the unease with which he'd read of this older woman's search to quench her sexual thirst and wondered what elements of his mother's own story were woven into it. Unlike her heroine, who'd experienced a sexual reawakening, the flings of Arfona's own grief had left her depressed and unsatisfied. The intensity of her feelings had been deepened by her inability to talk to anyone about them. She still felt a searing lack of intimacy in her life.

'I'll put the new chapter on your bed-side table,' Tecwyn answered his mother, handing her a drink. 'I'm going to take a shower.'

She smiled as he set the glass on the table beside the mound of peelings, saying, 'I'm looking forward to reading it!'

Uwe folded the dough over the sun dried tomatoes and worked the sticky mess for a few minutes, adding the odd fistful of flour until all the olive oil had been incorporated, and shaping it into two loaves. He knew already, from the feel of the dough, that the bread would be good. He set the loaves on the shelf above the Aga to prove.

'I'm having a shower now and then I'll take a nap until later on,' he told Arfona. 'There'll be time enough for everything else that we need to do.'

Uwe pushed into the steaming shower alongside Tecwyn and pulled himself against the hardness of his back, his hands exploring – stroking and touching. In all their years together, neither had tired of the delight they took in each other's bodies. Each was free to 'play'; they'd agreed in their first months that, given their respective histories with men, sexual fidelity would be irksome. It was a freedom they both valued, but never claimed, though neither knew it because each had agreed to spare the other the details. Tecwyn turned and they kissed deeply. And the sex they shared was good: it said '*Ich liebe dich... Rwy'n dy garu di...* I love you...' in ways that tired words in any language no longer could.

Through the half-sleep that came before the radio voices at five,

Tecwyn's certainty about the dinner party gave way to the misgivings Uwe had planted. Why was he being so solicitous? He had seen the seemingly endless queues of young women and girls who came to his clinics. Though their thoughtlessness and irresponsibility often made him depressed and angry, he sometimes envied their possibilities. And perhaps, deep within him, what he craved was the permission to realise such possibilities for himself. But whose permission? And he wept when he realised it was the permission he failed to grant to himself. Feeling suddenly vulnerable he pulled himself against Uwe and held him.

Arfona sank into the over-stuffed armchair in the bay window of the guest room; she liked its wallpaper and the view across the Dee and considered it her room whenever she stayed with the boys. She read the chapter her son had left on her bedside table. It irritated her that his Welsh was still not perfect. After all, he'd had the benefit of a Welsh language education – which was more than she could say for herself. She'd had to sit down and learn the grammar, making a conscious effort to use and write the language. She read with intense concentration, correcting the frequent errors but barely taking in the content of the piece. Only slowly did the awareness of Iolo Pawl's sexual experience dawn upon her. She wasn't shocked by what she'd read of these characters' antics. On realising, though, that the words and actions they described were conjured up by Tecwyn's imagination, she began to wonder if what he'd described were the kind of things he did with Uwe. It stung her that she'd begun to think about what her boys did sexually and she became uneasy. But curiosity displaced unease and she re-read the piece thinking all the time about Uwe and her son.

When she'd finished reading she looked out on the river, barely visible in the fading light, and sought to interpret her thoughts and feelings. She was mildly ashamed of what she felt was her voyeurism. Yet, putting this aside Arfona felt a certain liberation from a fear she had never fully realised. Reading her son's prose, she'd come to see that what two men might do together wasn't that much different from what she and her husband, Eifion had enjoyed. She smiled as she recalled the experimentation the sexual revolution of the 1960s had invited. They'd been sexually naive students at Bangor University then and the uninhibited exploration of one another's bodies had become their act of rebellion against the stifled sexual mores of their parents' generation. The thrill of Eifion's tongue on her clitoris for the first time... her first taste of his semen.... And she laughed quietly, remembering the student demonstration in London when they'd bought a dildo from a sex shop near Carnaby Street so that they could both feel what anal sex would be like before trying it out properly. The comfort of the armchair suddenly seemed to close over her... suffocating. Arfona Lewis yearned for her dead husband's lovemaking; she thanked whatever god that listened to silent prayers that Tecwyn and Uwe had each other.

Pouring more brandy over the pears and checking the loaves in the oven, Uwe wondered fleetingly if Arfona was becoming a bit unhinged. Coming down from her nap she'd given him the longest hug, a kiss, and said she loved him. It just wasn't her way. Her piano playing from the lounge hijacked his thoughts. Relishing the memory of a Chopin recital at the Bridgewater Hall he put the goose fat to warm and went down to the cellar to select the wines. Back in the kitchen he found Tecwyn sticking his fingers into pots and bowls, tasting, a crime punishable by finger amputation with the sharpest cleaver Uwe owned. Tecwyn left the kitchen in a hurry and went to check that there were enough fresh guest towels in the downstairs bathroom.

Richard and Penri were the first to arrive, immaculate, like models from some Paris autumn show. Close on their heels came Nick Bassham, all black leather and smiles, a tattoo of Celtic knot-work around his left wrist and not at all what Uwe had expected. As Tecwyn sorted their drinks, the phone rang; Tara and Mike would be late because the baby-sitter got the time wrong. Tecwyn winked at Uwe as he did his best imitation of a waiter and passed around the glasses: he'd won his bet again for those two were always late. Judith and Nia arrived; two beautiful women, elegant and understated, their skins tanned and hair sun-bleached after a holiday in Sri Lanka. And shortly after the appearance of the late arrivals, all moved into the dining room.

Much later, when they lay again in one another's arms, they un-picked the patchwork of the evening. Mike and Tara had talked about all the orphans the coalition against world terrorism had created. They saw a degree of madness in technological developments that made death for tens of thousands as unthinking a task as pressing the buttons on a dishwasher, and yet turned the creation of life itself into a well-refined laboratory technique.

Judith went on about how she'd acted for forty or fifty women, mostly lesbians, who'd made contracts with gay men in the few years since the successive New Labour administrations had changed the laws on surrogacy. The going rate was between thirty and fifty thousand Euros, plus expenses, and for some lesbian women it had been a way of tapping into the pink economy that had made so many gay men wealthy. Arfona had said something about love being all it takes to make a family, which was probably true but came out like trite drivel. Penri's preoccupation with designer things, from clothes to garden furniture, left no room in his and Richard's life for anything except the most chic; he kept interrupting the conversation with exaggerated compliments about their fine dining.

Uwe had liked Nick Bassham from Bodega Bay; he'd enjoyed

his stories. He was Californian, and fulfilled all the stereotypes. What other society, Uwe wondered, could produce a sperm-donating gay Episcopalian priest whose beautiful body was adorned with tattoos and piercings? An initial point of contact, Uwe's love of Hitchcock's *The Birds*, filmed at Bodega Bay, had sustained his interest in Nick throughout the dinner. Nick had presented the ethical objections to the recently licensed reproductive technologies as though delivering a three-point sermon. The humanitarian, the aesthetic and the religious were examined, and though Nick said nothing he and Tecwyn hadn't heard before, Uwe had appreciated his clarity.

Finally, tiring of their whispered conversation under the duvet, Tecwyn nuzzled closer into Uwe's cradling body and caught the musk of his warmth. It excited him. In time, Uwe sensed the rousing in Tecwyn and beckoned him. Their bodies moved over one another and in their communion Tecwyn knew what possibilities were theirs to be realised. Catrin would be a lovely name for a daughter... but would they spell it with a C or a K?

Between the Devil and the Virgin

Gareth sat with his back against the ramparts, eight hundred feet above the valley floor. He peered intently through squinted eyes into blurring haze, trying to identify the familiar landmarks. The golf course, bounded by the Dee, was obvious enough and knowing the line of the canal, that too took its place in the shimmering vista. Further east, where the narrow boats chugged for a fifth of a mile across Telford's aqueduct, a hundred and twenty feet above the river, not one of the nineteen arches were visible in the smudged Turner landscape. Up the valley to the west, the Cistercians had built their abbey in the Valley of the Cross, but a blotch of woodland concealed the ruins. His *nain* always called the place Llyn Egwestl. He could just make out the cottage where she'd been born and lived all her life. Remembering the Sunday teas, he felt himself slide even further into the pathos of nostalgic memories. He got to his feet and willed himself out of the self-pity that had tinged the edges of his day since breakfast.

To impress her mother, Beth-Ann had squeezed fresh orange juice and warmed a bag of Sainsbury's croissants. There was unsalted French butter, a jar of good blackcurrant jam and a box of deluxe muesli. Gareth quipped something about Aldi not being good enough anymore and she gave him a look that could kill, mouthing, 'Shut up and eat.' Louise pretended not to notice and became a loud American, effusive about her daughter's efforts and the sunshine streaming through the kitchen window. The coffee, dark and continental, had carried Gareth back to the café on the Piazza Anfiteatro in Lucca and a much happier time with Gwion. Louise distracted him, wanting to know what to look out for in Liverpool, but as their breakfast progressed Gwion broke through her prattling and Gareth felt the bleakness of their estrangement seep through him.

He declined Louise's invitation to go and be a tourist with them, thinking he'd be miserable company. As he washed up the breakfast dishes, though, he realised that being on his own all day would only make him feel more depressed and he began to regret his decision. Then the idea came to him that he could cycle himself out of it; strong physical exercise would get the hormones pumping around his body and lift his spirits. In less than an hour Gareth had crossed the bridge and was cycling along quiet country roads around the old estate to meet the lane that followed the river Clywedog up to Esclusham Mountain. There he'd take the forestry track to World's End.

It was a hot day. He stopped once by the river to quench his thirst and consider the remains of Offa's Dyke, which stood tall across the hillside before him, the evenly spaced trees along its ridge like sentries. Smearing his neck and legs with sun cream, he recalled the day that he and Gwion had rambled that section of the Dyke footpath with Beth-Ann and some of their friends from college. The memory darkened his mood, but he mounted his bike again, trying to put Gwion out of his mind. The steep pull up the mountain and the rough track across the moor were strenuous and crueller than he'd remembered, but he felt wonderfully alive from the physical effort and recognised his growing well-being. Gareth's thoughts flowed freely, settling here and there like insects. He hummed melodies in time to the rhythm of his pedalling and marvelled at the stonechats that sang from gorse bush perches, launching themselves occasionally into sky dances, their white collars and red breasts lucid against the gilded upland. Still the track took him higher to where the grouse chattered their distinctive 'go-back go-back' in the heather and a pair of peregrines soared, stooped and swooped. He stopped to watch their acrobatics and the muscles of his thighs and calves, jolted from their perpetual motion, twitched eagerly. On the crest of the open moor the sun was fierce. He thought of the forest; its shade seemed elusive, there on top of the world, but soon the fast and breezy descent brought him steeply down into the pine-scented coolness.

World's End gouged its course between Craig y Forwyn and Craig y Cythraul. Half way up the great limestone gorge, between the virgin and the devil, in amongst the relics of ancient mineshafts and limekilns, a spring bubbled up through the fallen boulders. Gareth knew it well from his childhood and splashing through the ford, where the stream from the spring crossed the track, he was thrilled to find it had not been parched by the hot, dry weather.

After hiding his bike in a clump of bracken he climbed up the gorge and found the pool, just below the spring, deep in the shadow of the soaring rocks. It was smaller than he remembered. He'd seen no one for more than an hour and feeling secure in his solitude he kicked off his trainers and peeled away the tee-shirt and shorts from his sweat soaked body. Reaching into the blue patch of sky above the gorge he stretched and tensed the muscle groups up and down his body, holding them taut and then slowly releasing the tightness. He repeated his cool-down a couple of times and was thrilled by the intense torrents of energy that surged through him. He brushed his nipples with the palms of his hands until each drupe hardened. Shocks sparked deeply, sending his body tingling. His right hand lingered at his chest, tracing the outlines of each firm pectoral, the fingers playing through the fine covering of hair. With his left hand he cupped his testicles, caressing them gently and intoxicating himself with the delight of it.... Then the coldness of the pool engulfed him. Gareth gasped for air.

Sobered by the cold penetrating his body, he lay on the grass for some time in a narrow shaft of sunlight. He bathed in its warmth until one persistent feeling invaded his calmness: the hunger for physical intimacy that had reawakened inside him. Gwion had been indifferent towards him for a while before their fight, not even wanting to cuddle. Gareth wondered if it really might be over; that in going away for the weekend to avoid him, Gwion was really telling him as much. He wanted so badly to say sorry and try to salvage their life together. But if Gwion had already made his decision to move on, where did that leave him?

The narrow lane from World's End wound tortuously between high hedges of blackthorn, elder and wild honeysuckle, with overhanging foxgloves and stinging nettles that rasped and nipped at his legs. His progress was slow, for the blind corners made hard cycling foolhardy, but his mind raced: Gwion; sex... the possibility of being single again. Running up to Castell Dinas Brân had been a whim; he'd thought that the adrenalin rush might just pull him from the doldrums.

Moving away from the ramparts, Gareth caught a glimpse of the boy; he sat in the shade cast by one of the few arches that had endured the centuries of battle, siege and neglect. Each time Gareth glanced in his direction the boy's eyes were on him. Anticipation and possibility stirred and provoked the desires that had welled up inside him at the pool. He glanced again – and again, each contact with the boy's eyes willed the prospect of intimacy. On the crown of a small rise, Gareth turned to face the boy, held his gaze, and smiled. The boy smiled and nodded.

They headed off towards the thicket where Gareth had hidden his bike, between two piles of forgotten fencing stakes long ago wrenched from the ground, when small fields went out of agricultural fashion. There were no courteous pleasantries:

'What do you like?' Gareth asked.

'This and that,' the boy said, with a trace of discomfort.

'I didn't bring any condoms,' Gareth said, gesturing that the boy take in the Lycra shorts and tee-shirt and realise he was on a cycle ride.

'I've got some, but I'm not sure I want to do that,' the boy said, unbuttoning his shirt and pulling it free from his shorts.

'Do you give, or take?'

'When it's okay... with the right person, I mean, then I like both.'

'I don't take it. I like to be fingered really gently... but nothing inside! Do you like to be sucked?'

Gareth noticed the line of hairs down from the boy's navel, cut sharply by the band of his shorts, and sensed his excitement at the prospect of what he'd find at their source.

'Yes,' the boy smiled, 'that's what I like best. And I like to suck too.'

In the cool heart of the thicket they stood naked before one another. The boy's kissing was eager, but his hands clumsy, touching and stroking Gareth where his own had explored and delighted earlier, by the pool. Gareth felt the boy's hardness on his thigh, then between his legs, joshing; teasing and delighting. And then the boy's tongue sucked at his nipple.

'I'm Gareth,' he whispered into the boy's ear.

'I'm Dan,' the boy whispered back.

Gareth's gluttony for the boy's body wasn't near to being sated when the grunted orgasm spilled, surprising and disappointing him. He drew away without looking at Gareth, reached into the long grass for his shorts and pulled them on. Gareth, spitting out the bitterest semen he'd ever tasted, felt the frustration rise through him and he blurted out, almost angrily, 'That's pretty selfish of you... just to leave me like this.' The boy looked startled and turned away.

And then, reaching for his own shorts, everything in Gareth's mind fractured into a sequence of frozen frames. Dan was bent low. He raised a stubby fencing picket above his head, holding it with both hands. He seemed to be yelling at him but all Gareth heard was a whisper: 'You fucking bastard of a cock-sucker.' Then the jolting shock of realisation and a dull pain as the stake splintered and shattered over him. Then the surprise in Dan's mean, blue eyes... the fear in his face as he turned and ran.

Gareth spat out spongy slivers of wood, pulpy and rotten. Time ceased as he picked a beetle from his pubic hair, the fragmented episode becoming only gradually animated in his daze. When the sequence of events began to flow with some coherence, he remained entirely still and imagined the whole of his body, sensing for the damaged and broken parts. The only soreness was around his right shoulder and over onto his chest. Almost imperceptibly he began to move the muscles and then rotate the whole joint. Only when certain that neither the clavicle nor scapula were broken did he look, and saw the reddish weal where the blow had struck. A small spider rooted amongst the fine, debris-strewn hairs on his chest.

Gareth heard the whispers and giggles from Beth-Ann's room and he wondered about disturbing them because he needed to talk. Cycling back from Llangollen, the encounter with Dan had been re-wound and played over and over. His first thought, still in the depth of the thicket as he'd dressed, avoiding the soreness in his shoulder, was that he'd provoked Dan. He'd tried to remember exactly what he'd said to the boy as he'd pulled away... how threatening had he seemed? Later, as he cycled, more sinister interpretations took shape in his mind. He needed to get another viewpoint, to put a check on his paranoia. He hesitated before knocking on Beth-Ann's door. Did he really want her to know he'd been so casual? Perplexed in his hesitation, he decided to shower. Under the jets of water that soothed his bruised shoulder, Gareth thought of Rhodri, an old lover. His training as a police officer would surely help to untangle the embellishments of his imagination and see the event for real. He felt sure, too, that Rhodri would be able to offer him consolation in ways that Beth-Ann might not consider.

They sat at a small table in a bay window with a view of the river. Rhodri, dark and thick set, drank his coffee, his left hand cradling his weekend stubbled chin. He flicked his left earlobe unconsciously, his index finger nicely manicured but crooked. Gareth smiled, remembering the endearing habit, and slurped the last of the Ferry Inn's house red from the over-large wine glass.

'I'd really like it if you'd come home with me,' Rhodri ventured.

'That would be nice,' Gareth said, still attracted to him and moved by the concern he'd shown. The stirring in his groin made him remember how good they'd once been together.

'Do have a think about what I said then,' Rhodri urged, pressing his knee momentarily against the inside of Gareth's thigh in a gesture of reassurance before nudging it upwards provokingly. 'If you want me to talk to one of the liaison officers in the Community Protection Unit, just let me know. This kind of thing needs investigating, really. The next time this guy decides to hit someone over the head he might just do some real harm. Think hard on that, Gareth, please. Just imagine how you'd feel if his next victim....'

'I know that I should report it, Rhod,' Gareth interrupted. Rhodri's knee pressed gently again, the gesture calming.

'I can't really risk drawing that sort of attention to myself though, not in the kind of work I do,' Gareth said, playing his fingers over Rhodri's knee. 'It's all right for New Labour to have gays and lesbians in their London cabinet, but look what happened in the Assembly? And around here, you know as well as I do, that sort of thing just won't wash.'

'Probably all the other men this weirdo has attacked feel the same way, so we don't ever get enough information to build up a case against him.'

'Yea... yea... yea... so what is it about North Wales Police that's keeping your closet door so tightly shut?' Gareth jibed. 'Put the shoe on the other foot, Rhodri and tell me what you'd do.'

His silence confirmed Gareth's suspicion that the police did not easily perceive the gap between their own professional advice and personal practice.

For fifteen, maybe twenty minutes they lay together, exhausted in a sexually sated slumber. Gareth felt a residual dribble from Rhodri's shrunken cock; it trickled down his thigh, tickling, but he couldn't reach down to wipe it away because Rhodri lay across him. To distract himself he thought about the events that had led him to fall so willingly into Rhodri's arms: the stupid row with Gwion... the pent-up sexual frustration and his fling in the bushes with Dan that had left him bruised and shaken. Rhodri farted and Gareth sensed the shallowness of their intimacy. Feeling awfully alone, he wanted to be held by Gwion – and no one else.

Mischief and Deep Secrets

Morfudd Jones rocked the soggy stub of her third cigarette into a clean, pale blue patch of the Wedgwood ashtray – the one that Alwena Jones had given her for her birthday the previous September. It had come from a small but treasured collection of Jasperware, which Alwena displayed on the Victorian chiffonier in her room. Before, Morfudd had always used a heavy glass one that the home had grudgingly provided... though Matron generally disapproved and had made her promise that she wouldn't smoke in bed. After a sigh – that might have summed up how tiresome she found this awakening before five, or was perhaps just an expression of the disdain she felt at another day being added to the thirty odd thousand days she'd already endured – she wiped the drool that had dribbled down her chin onto her wizened breast with a crumpled tissue and heaved her stiff legs from beneath the covers. The first few steps were always a bit of a wobble now, but with a hand on the bedside table and the smooth curving mahogany of the vitrine that held her last few precious knick-knacks, she eventually steadied herself. With a straight back, she walked into the bay and pulled back the curtains.

It had rained again in the night: July was proving to be a washout. The Pines Rest Home stood on an exposed outcrop above the town, taking all the weather blown in off Cardigan Bay. Morfudd sulked at the wild, white stallions that charged onto

144

the sandy beach beyond the council houses and the heavy, grey clouds that closed the town in on itself. Perching herself on the arm of the easy chair where she sometimes sat to watch the life of the town through a pair of cracked binoculars, she started to day-dream. It was only when her red-ringed, rheumy eyes fell on the crescent rose bed in the front garden below her window that she remembered Buddug Jones.

Morfudd stood and looked around the large, airy room for the plastic carrier bag that she'd put down the evening before. She'd been affected when Buddug had become so upset by the wet weather ruining the roses and had persuaded Matron to let her go down into town in the van with Griff, but only on condition that she came back up in a taxi. Matron was like that; always extracting promises and setting conditions. She'd tried Woolworth and the flower shop by the station, and even ventured into the Bargain Centre in the old *Capal Wesla* – and to think they were selling pan scourers and German condoms on the very spot where the *Parchedig* Tomos Talfan Elias had christened both her boys. Feeling downhearted, Morfudd had nipped into the wine store and bought a bottle of Grouse so that her jaunt wouldn't be completely in vain. But then, on a stall in the market, run by an Indian woman with a spot of paint on her forehead and wearing jeans under her sari, she'd found what she'd been looking for. After her adventure in town, she'd feigned an overwhelming fatigue for the remainder of the day and closed herself in her room, leaving Alwena and Buddug to their soaps and their knitting. She'd ruined her nail scissors during the afternoon trimming a good foot off each of the stiff, plastic stems and cutting three-inch lengths from the roll of green garden wire. She spied the carrier bag nuzzled against the vitrine and with a sharp intake of breath she set about her little spot of gardening.

After placing the stupidly grimacing gnome from beside the pot of geraniums against the open front door so as not to lock herself out, Morfudd Jones set off across the lawn. The grass was soggy and it squelched between her gnarled toes. For a fleeting moment she wondered what the casual observer of her early morning expedition might conclude. Hesitating, she considered the wisdom of retracing her steps and changing from her nightdress, but then concluded that she should press on to the rose bed and get on with the job. On the stems that George, the handy man, had already dead-headed, Morfudd attached the short-stalked buds and blooms, pricking her fingers, hands and forearms as she bound the green garden wire tightly around the overlapping ends. Fixing the roses took much longer than she'd anticipated but no one interrupted her and she was back in her room by five to six.

Over the past months, Alwena Jones and Buddug Jones had both stopped putting on make-up, which saved them ten minutes in the mornings. They were already looking into their tea when Morfudd came into the dining room. It was Alwena's idea, to stop smoothing away the wrinkles with foundation and powder: '*Duw,* it's time we stopped plastering Polyfilla into the cracks... time to grow old disgracefully,' she'd coaxed. Buddug, being the most weak-willed of the three, had followed suit after a short time. Morfudd, commenting frequently that they both looked like death warmed up, remained faithful to her Seamless Liquid Foundation in porcelain and her Sun Frolic crème puff, but her enthusiastic attempts to disguise the ravages of age often led to grotesque consequences. As Morfudd poured herself a cup of tea, Alwena noticed all the scratches from the rose bushes.

'You had your hands in Joseff-*Fferm*'s ferret bag?' she goaded.

Morfudd smiled, answering, 'I've been sewing the buttons back onto my winter coat after it came back from the dry cleaners.' Buddug, who was more than a little deaf, said that her Michael was coming for tea.

'I hope he'll bring me some roses – that rain has spoiled all the ones in the crescent bed. Maybe he'll bring some Welsh cakes from Corner Café too!'

Alwena raised her eyes to the gods and wondered if senility was infectious. Morfudd peered between the two women, whose backs were to the window, and beamed at the crescent rose bed where the Deep Secrets and the Mischief swayed in the breeze off the sea.

'Your Michael is such a good boy, coming to see you like he does,' she remarked, remembering the hundreds of Marlboro's he'd given her when he and his *friend* had resolved to give up smoking. The smile got lost in the slobbery burlesque line of Max Factor's Firebrand and her eyes dimmed beneath the smudged aquamarine eye shadow. She couldn't remember when her surviving son had last called to see her.

A while later, as Buddug and Alwena disagreed over an instruction in the knitting pattern, Morfudd wondered what had kept her Aled away for so long. She knew that being a solicitor was an important, busy job – and he and Melissa had, after all, seen to it that she was in a *private* rest home... though why she couldn't have gone into their granny flat was beyond her. Wasn't that what granny flats were for? But then, Melissa had her aerobics and her golf – and all her commitments on *the bench*. Feeling herself becoming despondent, she straightened her back and thought about how effeminately ridiculous Buddug's Michael was. It was a disgrace, how lovey-dovey he and his friend were. And thinking it was better to have no visitors at all than to be visited by ones quite so queer, she felt her spirits rise again.

When Michael and Gerard arrived just before three-thirty, with roses for Buddug, Welsh cakes for tea and a box of Thornton's for sharing around, Morfudd lifted her copy of *People's Friend* to within inches of her nose and made believe she hadn't noticed them... but she peeked now and then, and strained to hear their conversation. Michael, whom she dismissed as a balding, bulging, blubbering milksop, fussed for the first ten minutes over his mother's hearing aid – well, over the fact that she wasn't wearing it again – whilst Gerard, who looked so much like Gregory Peck, talked with Alwena about the latest twists and turns in *Coronation Street*. Morfudd could make herself feel quite sick if she thought too much about how indiscreet these boys could be, but sometimes she allowed her curiosity to get the better of her and she'd wonder which of the two wore the frocks and pinafores about the bungalow they lived in together. Gerard looked so manly that she couldn't conceive of him being the wife!

'I thought you said the roses in the front had been ruined with all the rain, Mam,' Morfudd overheard Michael saying with a barb of accusation as he fussed, arranging the bunch of roses he'd brought his mother in a tall jam pot that one of the girls handed him as an excuse for a vase: 'You've no need to be telling me porkies to get me to bring you flowers, you know.' With this, Morfudd closed her magazine, wiped the ooze from her chin, and waited for events to unfold.

'But they are all spoiled,' Buddug insisted, getting up with some difficulty and hobbling over to the window. 'Poor George, who's taken such a lot of care with them, was out there yesterday – but....'

'See,' Michael said with a full-of-himself 'I told you so'.

'*Brenin y bratiau*,' Buddug exclaimed, the astonishment causing her to stagger and reach for the arm of Miss Perkins' chair to steady herself, 'but only yesterday... I watched poor George dead-heading them.'

'That wasn't yesterday Buddug *fach*,' Morfudd put in mischievously, knowing that she could sometimes get a bit mixed up. 'We both sat here watching George one afternoon last week...

not yesterday. Come and sit down and open these chocs.'

'How are you then Morfudd love?' Michael asked, guiding his mother back to her chair, his voice at too high a pitch, its modulation too singsong. Morfudd hated it that he called her love all the time, and that he was so brazen to think he could be on first name terms with her. 'Not getting you all excited is it, love... that *People's Friend*? They tell me it's got quite a reputation for saucy stories.'

'But it's been raining for days,' Buddug said, her surprise giving way to an upset bewilderment, 'and roses never do well in the rain.'

'Come on Mam,' Michael encouraged. 'Sit down here and we'll all have a nice cup of tea.'

'Oh – but they are lovely,' Buddug said, turning to appreciate the roses in the crescent bed before Michael coaxed her back to her chair, where she sat, her head skewed awkwardly, trying to keep sight of them through the blur of cataracts. Morfudd sipped her tea and enjoyed the buttery taste of the cakes – and she feasted for a while on Buddug's childlike pleasure.

Before the gong went for dinner, Alwena Jones noticed the commotion outside. By the crescent rose bed, Kylie, one of the girls who came in to wash the dishes during the school holidays was screeching with laughter, while George leaned on his garden fork and scratched his head. Matron, bent low over a rose bush, was picking at a rosebud as if it was a dog's stinking turd, by the look on her face. Alwena roused Buddug and Morfudd from their magazines.

'I want them all taken off, George,' came Matron's hysterical entreaty through the open window.

'What's she saying to George then?' Buddug quizzed. 'Oh, they look so cheap and nasty,' Matron harangued. 'Our residents here at the Pines don't pay for any kind of imitation, George...

this isn't what you'd expect at a *private rest home* – you've been here long enough to know that.' She held open a black plastic bin liner and gestured to him: 'I want every one of them off, now!'

Buddug began to wail when she saw George and Matron vandalise the crescent rose bed. Alwena, though confused by what she was witnessing, leaned over and took Buddug's hand to comfort her. Morfudd, feeling Buddug's distress, got up from her chair and after steadying herself, walked to the window and rapped her knuckles hard against the pane until she captured the vandals' attention.

'Please stop that, Matron,' she called through the open window with a determination that surprised Morfudd herself. 'Those roses are giving Buddug, Alwena and me such pleasure. Stop it immediately.'

'But they're *plastic roses* Mrs Jones,' Matron sallied forth, 'artificial... not real.'

'But from here they look beautiful Matron... and when you're over eighty, and your world has shrunk to the four walls of an *old people's home*, a little bit of beauty isn't a lot to ask for – even when it is an imitation.'

'Mrs Jones *fach*, we're a *private rest home* –.'

'And private means that *we* are paying, doesn't it Matron?' Morfudd interrupted with all the sharpness that her drooling tongue could cut, 'so Buddug, Alwena and I would like you to leave the plastic roses just the way they are.'

And the plastic roses in the crescent bed swayed on in the evening breeze.

Morfudd Jones and Alwena Jones watched the orange streaks fade in the sky over Bardsey Island and waited for the last of the less mobile residents to be escorted to their bedrooms. When they were finally alone, Morfudd poured a good joch of whisky into each of their cocoa stained mugs from the flask she kept in her handbag.

'You do some lovely things to keep Buddug's spirits up,' Alwena offered by way of thanks as Morfudd passed her the mug.

'She's had so much disappointment in her life,' Morfudd said, 'especially the way that Michael of hers has turned out.'

'But he comes to see her, Morfudd *fach*, which is more than I can say for any of my three,' Alwena answered.

'My Aled comes when he can,' Morfudd countered with an eagerness that betrayed her disillusionment. She wiped the spit from her chin and took a slug of whisky.

'Do you think about your Lewis sometimes?' Alwena asked after a while. 'Now he was a lovely boy. He and our Nesta were very thick for a time... remember?'

'I never think about him!' Morfudd spat, and hoped that her tears would drown in her watery eyes.

'*Duw* – it's such a different world now,' Alwena mused.

'You see them in the magazines all the time; boys with boys and girls with girls....'

Morfudd took another slug of whisky. Its fiery sharpness couldn't raze the memory of finding her Lewis hanging from a beam in the attic just hours after his father had bawled that no son of his –.

'Gerard was even telling me this afternoon that they've been accepted by the adoption panel,' Alwena interrupted Morfudd's thoughtfulness. 'They're hoping to make Buddug a *nain* before Christmas; now won't that be nice for her?'

Morfudd swallowed her revulsion and tried hard to force a smile.

Gifts

I watched Rhun as he skimmed through the glut of Christmas post. Among the round robins, those often meagre attempts to sum up 'the year in the life of' were those from people we didn't particularly care about and hadn't seen for years. These he tossed aside after only a perfunctory glance. Some of the Christmas cards, however, brought smiles and joyful sighs. About half way through the stack he took a slurp of wine and quipped, 'No surprises this year then?' He might have been anticipating a greeting from someone we'd lost touch with whose company we'd enjoyed or someone we'd fallen out with over something totally inane, but I knew he was thinking of an evening just like this exactly a year ago.

Krista's letter had arrived in an elastic-banded bundle. It was on the day I'd been looking out for Dewi-post to give him his Christmas box. Because my parents were coming to us for the holiday I'd taken a couple of days off work to clean the house (my mother is such a fastidious woman). I'd watched Dewi trudge up the lane through the sludge of the previous day's snow. He looked perished so I asked him in for a coffee or something – like you do at Christmas. He only stayed long enough to gulp down his tea: although he was curious enough about us, he was clearly uncomfortable to be alone in the house with me.

I must have read Krista's letter half a dozen times. The fact that she'd deteriorated so quickly left me wondering if she'd skipped a year and the news of her daughter's coming out was already two years old. I hadn't known that diabetes could knacker your kidneys. The dialysis sounded awful and the wait for a kidney even more wearing. They'd been down the route of looking to her immediate family to see if one of them could donate. Phil, her husband, had high blood pressure and Hannah, like her mother, was diabetic. There was a brother who'd joined the Jehovah's Witnesses, so he hadn't even been asked to consider a blood test. So she was on a waiting list. She sometimes found herself daydreaming, especially around Bank Holidays and Christmas, that some wonderfully fit and healthy person would be fatally injured on the road so that she might regain her life. Waking from such daydreams, she'd come out in a cold sweat realising what a nightmare she was wishing on some anonymous family.

Throughout that day as I hoovered and dusted, made up the spare bed (I even ironed the sheets and pillowcases), bleached the loo and zapped the black scummy mould in the shower with stuff from one of those spray guns, I thought about Krista. We'd had a lot of fun together, and a lot of heartache too... half a lifetime ago.

Aberystwyth in the late seventies. We met at Welsh classes. I'd got it into my head that since I'd come to Wales to study I ought to learn my granny's mother tongue. I had little understanding of what I was taking on. Krista's motive seemed more lofty; she was into Celtic languages. She was into Abba and disco too... a real dancing queen. In those days it wasn't so easy to come out but by the middle of the first term Krista had sussed me. Walking down Penglais Hill one Saturday night after the disco in the union bar she asked me straight out. The alcohol had loosened both our tongues and by the time we reached the prom I was in floods of tears. Southport wasn't exactly the best place for a gay boy to grow up and come to understand himself. I was still very confused and still very much a virgin. We sat in a shelter by the bandstand for ages, just talking.

There was a sense of covertness about the Aber Gay Soc. There was no phone number, just a PO box in the old union building. Krista helped me write the letter. I didn't want it to sound too pathetic. It took more than a week for anyone to respond. I was invited to meet two of the members in the front bar of the Belle Vue... I could bring a friend if I wanted to. Krista held my hand.

I fell head over heels with Patrick and we had an intense couple of months. Krista consoled me when he went off with Jimmy. On the re-bound I found myself in bed with Hugh, one of the lecturers from organic chemistry, who must have been at least forty (though he kept himself in good shape). It was in the days after that frantic night of lusty tumble that I learned the meaning of the term chicken queen: Hugh liked them young and wasn't looking for love and I was just another weekend treat from the meat counter. Then Owain screwed me over and screwed me up and I started to hate gay life in Aberystwyth and wonder if it would always be that way.

That summer after our first year Krista and I went inter-railing. Every other night we slept on a train to save money. We managed a month in Europe, nine countries, fifteen big cities and one decent meal a day on a hundred and twenty-five quid each, money we'd saved from our grants. On the nights we stayed in hostels and cheap hotels, we shared a room and shared a bed, and whether it was something about being in foreign lands, or something in the air, we slept together. Well, more than just slept, I mean.

We carried on after the summer break, but back in Aber it didn't seem so romantic or so real somehow. Shagging on a single bed in the halls of residence, where you could hear everything through the walls, seemed to bring a different world upon us and being in familiar surroundings made me think again about being gay. A couple of weeks into the term I was seeing Tudor and feeling bad about two-timing Krista. Then, on a Wednesday in early November she said she'd missed her period. What did I know about contraception? I'd just assumed she'd sorted it. I behaved like a real shit. I even asked her if she was sure it was mine. We didn't see one another for ages after the abortion.

On a Saturday in January we bumped into one another in Galloway's and I persuaded her to come to the Cabin for a coffee. We talked and then walked the prom to kick the bar. She'd started seeing someone. I said I was glad. I also said I was sorry for all the hurt I'd caused her. She said she'd missed being friends with me. I said we could still be friends if she wanted, but it didn't happen. When we met, in the union refec or the back bar of the Skinners, we'd agree that we should do something together, but we never did.

A good few years after we'd graduated and moved on from Aber I saw her in a restaurant in Manchester. I was with Roger, an architect, the only married man I ever went out with. She was with a handsome, blond man and they looked all intimate, so I decided it would be better not to renew our acquaintance, but she caught my eye as we got up to leave. So I met Phil. They were celebrating their fourth wedding anniversary. We swapped addresses, but I didn't expect to hear from her. The next Christmas I got the first of her newsy round robins.

After cleaning all day and making a beef casserole ready for when Rhun got home, I lounged in the bath and wondered whether it was even possible for a live stranger to donate a kidney. Setting the table for dinner I stuffed Krista's letter into the middle of the heap so as not to draw attention to it and rehearsed the lines I might say to Rhun. He laughed, which really put me off my stride, and said that the chances of a cross match were so remote that I should save myself the bother. I said that if the chances were really so remote he wouldn't mind if I got a leaflet from the transplant centre in Liverpool.

Beryl George, the transplant coordinator, spoke to me via the switchboard.

'Live non-related donors aren't that common in Britain, but it happens a lot in America. I'll put some information in the post for you.' She continued, 'The first step would be to have a blood test to see if you've the same blood group as Krista. Make an appointment later on if you want to move things on.'

I found the card from the Blood Transfusion Service in an old wallet full of bits and pieces. Before the whole AIDS thing, I'd given blood regularly but then they started advising those of us in high-risk groups against doing so. O positive. Then I went to the top floor of the Royal Liverpool Hospital to meet Beryl. Rhun pooh-poohed it all as a waste of her time and mine, but she took me very seriously. There was me thinking I was going for a bit of a chat and she says she might as well check me out. Weight... height... blood pressure... medical history... and some blood tests, just to check for a hundred and one things as well as any infectious diseases.

'Do you mean AIDS and stuff?' I asked.

'There's no point raising your friend's hopes if you're unsuitable from the word go because of things like CMV, Hepatitis B, Hepatitis C or HIV.'

She gave me a couple of two litre containers and an instruction sheet to take away with me.

Rhun was hostile: 'Are you going through a mid-life crisis?

Why else would you want to do something so fucking crazy for someone who's practically a stranger?'

I answered him cautiously, 'Once upon a time, in another life, I loved Krista. Perhaps, if you've loved someone once, they stay a bit special, you know?' It sounded trite and untrue, especially when I thought of all the men in my life. But that was the first time Rhun knew that Krista was more than just someone I'd known in Aber.

Beryl phoned to say that all the blood tests had come back and they were fine. I'd passed the first hurdle and it was now an appropriate time to put my offer to Krista. I looked them up in our Christmas card address book and wrote her a letter. She phoned me less than an hour after she'd torn the envelope open. She was O positive too... and did I really know what I was letting myself in for?

We started e-mailing. She wanted me to be open and honest with her, every step of the way. If I was going to embark on this journey she wanted all the gory details so that she could share it with me... and she wanted to know what I was thinking. And if I changed my mind it would be alright... she'd understand. Some of our e-mails were plain stupid. *You and Phil sure you're okay about a gay kidney*, I fired off one day. *Of course*, came the reply, *as long as it's healthy and working well... it'll give a whole new meaning to being gay friendly!*

Beryl made an appointment for me with the consultant physician and nephrologist and made the arrangements for more bloods that could be sent for cross matching with Krista's. I had to say something at work because I needed time off to drive to Liverpool. My boss said it was a noble thing I was doing, embarrassing me. The news came through that the match, though not perfect, was good enough, especially given that kidneys from live donors were preferable to ones from cadavers.

157

If I wanted to go on I'd have to have an IVP and a renal artereogram, invasive procedures that required someone to accompany me to the hospital. Beryl suggested that perhaps Rhun would come with me: she wanted a chat with him.

As the weeks passed, Rhun had begun to realise that the chances were looking better and he'd stopped joking about it... in fact, he'd stopped talking about it altogether. When I asked him if he'd come with me to the hospital, the real possibility of it all hit him. He went ballistic.

'Why are you being so selfish?' he exploded. 'Don't I matter anymore? Don't you care what I think about it all... what I'm feeling? What if something goes wrong? Why d'you have to do this?'

I tried to articulate it. With Beryl it hadn't seemed so difficult but with Rhun I couldn't find words. 'So you think you owe it to her, like repaying a bad debt?' he asked. I tried to explain what our relationship had been like... and the abortion. Being a gay man in my forties... no kids... leaving no real impression on the world... leaving nothing behind. What was happening with Krista was important and I had the opportunity to make a real difference in somebody's life.

Very quietly, Rhun said, 'And you don't think you've made a real difference in my life?'

There were a few horrible days. I'd failed to explain my motives and Rhun curled up in his spiky shell and closed me out. The appointment card came through for the IVP. It was a glorious Saturday morning in May and we'd planned a hike up the Rhinogs.

'What if you can't go on rambles afterwards?' Rhun quizzed with less hostility and more concern.

'Maybe, if you came with me,' I said, gesturing towards the appointment card, 'Beryl or Dr Williams would be able to answer your questions.' He blew me a kiss across the table, responding more soberly, 'I don't want you to do this, but I have to respect your right to follow it through. I'll arrange to take the day off.'

The IVP was fine: a shot of dye in the arm and a series of X-rays that showed the venous structure of the kidneys. Beryl had her chat with Rhun, and in the next days he opened up much more. He downloaded articles that we discussed at length, especially the testimonies of those who'd donated kidneys. He seemed satisfied that the recovery rate for the donor was very good and that the one remaining kidney had the capacity to grow and compensate for the other.

'Beryl said that unless I was a hundred percent behind you she'd pull the plug on the whole thing,' Rhun ventured one afternoon as we dug up potatoes. I asked him what had made him change his mind.

'A person willing to give a kidney to a friend is a pretty special kind of person and it's made me love you even more. Though I still think you're off your head!'

The renal artereogram was the last hurdle. A fine catheter was inserted under local anaesthetic into an artery in my groin, and then coaxed up towards the kidneys. Once in position, a dye was released to show the arterial structure of the kidneys. Some people have two arterial branches serving one or even both kidneys and that makes them unsuitable for removal; mine had one artery each. Lying flat on my back as still as possible for four hours afterwards was a bore. Rhun read the newspaper, flirted with the nurse who checked my blood pressure every twenty minutes and then went off to have lunch with Beryl.

The thumbs up came through in August and the surgery was set for the first Thursday in September. Work had given me a three-month paid special leave and as the news got around people stopped me in the corridors and in the canteen to say how brave... selfless... virtuous... and just plain fucking stupidly wonderful I was.

'You'd do the same for someone you loved,' I'd fire back at them. 'You would, wouldn't you?' And sometimes you could see it in their faces that they bloody well wouldn't.

The surgeon came around a couple of hours after I'd been admitted. He was younger than I'd expected. He talked with Rhun and me for a while, referring back to the notes he'd been sent from the Royal Liverpool. Then he did a physical examination and took my blood pressure.

'You're a bit anxious I expect,' he said as he noted the numbers on my chart. He scanned the notes from Liverpool again. 'There's no history of high blood pressure in your family is there?' With some puzzlement I said that there wasn't, as far as I knew, and wondered whether it was the fact that he was so fancyable that had excited me. He did the test again a few minutes on, and looked perplexed as he wrote the numbers down. Then he got someone else to do it and it was higher again. It levelled out by the middle of the afternoon at 180 over 120... and that's where it hovered for the three days that I stayed in the hospital.

I was depressed for about a month after my attempt to donate was aborted. Of course, Krista and Phil were gutted to have come so close, only to have all their hopes thwarted, but they were so nice with me. Rhun was wonderfully tender and kept assuring me that despite the thoughts in my head and the desires of my heart, my body finally said a very definite no... and that that was alright. I became preoccupied with notions of failure and for the first time in my life I questioned whether it was indeed better to have tried and failed than not to have tried at all. By the middle of October my blood pressure settled back down at 130 over 80 and I went back to work. People were kind and I tried to get back to normal.

Rhun must have said something to Krista and Phil about those bleak days. She sent me a letter, which arrived one austere November day.

You must think about what you have given to me and Phil, and not think about what couldn't in the end be given. I've grown used to being let down by my body over the years. Count yourself lucky that the way in which your body let us all down hasn't caused you any long-term physical harm. I know that you're upset, but please know and understand that the gifts you gave me this past year are priceless. You renewed my faith in the depth and breadth of friendship, you restored my trust in loyalty, you showed us kindness the like of which is never forgotten... and most of all you gave me something to hope for.

Rhun took another slurp of wine and reached for my parents' Christmas card, which I'd shoved towards the bottom of the bundle. Their Christmas gift to us, a cheque for five thousand pounds, fluttered to the floor as he opened it.

'I thought you said there were no surprises this year,' he said with a hint of accusation.

The View from Sasso Fermo

The impressive fountain churned up in the wake of the twin-hulled *Carducci* quickly washed away the view of the landing stage, the palm trees and the boxes of mauve geraniums that adorned the wall along the lakefront promenade. Out of breath, Glain gripped the handrail to steady herself against the ferryboat's roll but as the surge of acceleration unbalanced her she slipped her arm through Cai's. Her silver streaked hair blew in all directions and the three points of the Hermes silk scarf tied around her neck flapped with manic indignity.

'We made it,' she said after catching her breath, her voice rasping from too many cigarettes. 'I really thought that we'd miss it and have to wait for the six-o-clock.'

Cai smiled. It was the first time in many months that Glain had seen him smile and it made her more optimistic.

Once the boat had reached its cruising speed it was stable in the water and the passengers could walk about the deck with less caution. Glain began to relax and she spoke with a man in a white linen jacket who'd begun to show an interest in her. Cai moved to the side rail, leaned against its metallic smooth coolness, and gazed at the forested mountains that rose steeply from the water's edge. Seeing the ridges and gorges emerge from the afternoon shadows as the boat made its swift progress along the lake, he was eager to hike the trails he'd studied on maps the reception manager at the Villa Cannero had agreed to send when Glain had made their booking. In profile Cai was handsome: clear skin, a small, slightly pointed nose, the eye more grey than blue, which from a certain angle was shot through with turquoise, and jet-black hair worn almost cropped. He drew the wondering glances of men and women in equal measure.

Half smiling at the man along the rail to his right who'd begun to cruise him, Cai unconsciously drew his hand across the stubble of his left cheek before resting his chin in its wide palm. Even when closely shaven, his beard was dark and this pronounced the clean, white line, more surgical than accidental, that ran through his top lip, just up from the left corner of his mouth, and forged across his cheek to within a centimetre of his eye. It was impossible not to notice. It was what most people – strangers, even those initially attracted to his right profile – saw before turning away. The few not put off by such disfigurements, like Tudor, could see that the scar added interest, and even some mystery to a face that the bitchier queens on the scene would have said was pretty.

Most of those who didn't turn away were still too embarrassed to acknowledge it... but Tudor had asked about the scar straight away. His forthright manner had taken me aback, but he had a way of putting you at ease. The first time we slept together he drew his fingers gently over it, 'kissed it better' and ran his tongue along its length. Even then, all those years ago, Tudor seemed to know about human fragility and understood that broken people needed a little extra gentleness. After we'd moved in together 'kissing it better' became a bit of a goodnight ritual.

'This is Max,' Glain said, interrupting Cai's imaginary ramble in the mountains. 'He's staying at Villa Cannero too.'

'Hello,' Max said with enthusiasm.

'Hi,' Cai said, turning towards them. He offered the man in

the white linen jacket the broadest smile and began to think that perhaps Max might be his saviour. What had ever possessed him to come away with Glain?

Max flinched. He was unable to disguise the wince that momentarily twisted his photogenic features. He averted his gaze, focussed on the small Celtic cross that Cai wore on a chain around his neck, and said the first thing that came into his head: 'Glain was just telling me how much she's looking forward to making a trip down to the Borromeo islands and maybe spending a morning at the market in Cannobio.'

Sensing Max's embarrassment, Cai put his arm through Glain's and teased her: 'You were reading the guide book all the way over on the flight... weren't you Mam?'

'Don't be so damn cheeky Cai,' Glain said with a laugh in her voice. 'I married your father but I was never your Mam. He's only eight years younger than me see, Max... I was married to a much older man.'

'I'm sorry,' Max said, laughing, 'I'd just assumed that you were a couple.' Cai sensed too that he was sorry for the way he'd flinched.

'Well, ' Glain said, 'we're on a 'singles' holiday... but it's so horrible to sit and eat on your own – or have to share a table with strangers who've never seen a fish knife in their lives. We decided to come away together, but to do our own thing and still have one another's company at meal times.'

'I know exactly what you mean,' Max confided. 'This is my first holiday on my own... since the divorce.'

'And are you planning to do all those touristy things then, Max... the islands and the Villa Taranto?' Cai quizzed, seeing a plan come together.

'Isn't that why people come to Lago Maggiore?' Max asked with a shrug.

'So maybe, when I go off hiking,' Cai ventured, 'you two might keep one another company?'

'And you could eat with us, Max,' Glain said with an open armed gesture that perhaps said more than she'd intended about her own wishful thinking. 'We can be a ménage!'

'But are you sure I know how to use a fish knife?' Max quizzed, with a sparkle of mischief in his eyes.

When I first met Tudor he'd been on a fairly tough fitness regime for about a year. He was still big. When he took off his clothes you could see that he was still fat and that his skin was loose, even saggy, from where the five stones had been lost. He was older... quite a bit older really, but it didn't seem to matter. After we'd been together a couple of years he was down to thirteen stone and still working out. It was about that time that I became quite insecure for a while... once he'd got himself into such good shape and was looking like a film star. No fitness regime was going to sort out my face: no amount of kisses would make it better and we couldn't afford cosmetic surgery.

'It's quite a sight, don't you think?' Max volunteered as the boat turned towards the shore. 'The people who recommended I come here said that the ferry was the best way to approach Cannero for the first time.'

'It's beautiful... and that must be the Villa Cannero,' Glain said, pointing at the yellow and white palace to the right of the jetty, its balconies heavy with pink geraniums, its lawned terraces stepped down to the water's edge.

'I think I'm going to be pleased that we paid for a balcony and a lake view,' Cai said, remembering the argument he'd had with Glain over all the supplements; the single room surcharge alone was outrageous.

*It took a long time for me to understand that Tudor loved me...
perhaps because I don't know, even to this day, if I loved him. He said
– once, when he was pissed off with me because I kept doubting him
– that the chip on my shoulder was more repellent than the scar on
my face... but that the chip, at least, was something I could work on.*

After the last of the grand villas, high above the village, the
cobbled track ended abruptly. Rough steps, hewn into the rock,
led to a steep path that quickly yielded panoramas of the lake,
which shimmered in the morning heat, taking Cai's breath away.
The gradient soon exhausted his awe at the views and his startled
amazement at the zucchini-fat lime-green lizards that skited into
the undergrowth from sun-soaked slabs of granite. Stopping now
and then for long draughts of rosemary-scented air, he watched
butterflies – some a silky black, many more common yellows, and
the rare few with blood red wing tips. He was amazed too by the
hydrangeas – banks and banks purple, indigo and pink, like
surreal cotton wool clouds that had fallen from the sky and come
to rest on the mountainside.

After a three-hour climb, Cai ate bread and cheese, and drank
some rough local wine, at an *osteria* in Cheglio. The youth that
seemed to be in charge had a square face, although there were no
hard corners. A light beard softened the lines of his jaw and waves
of sun-streaked hair crested onto the wide strand of his forehead.
When he smiled his cheeks puffed and his eyes danced: a lapis
gem in the lobe of his right ear drew attention away from their
gaze. His smile revealed beautiful teeth between lips that were
fleshy. Cai watched him pout as he supped beer from a bottle.
Then, distracted by another customer, the smile faded and the
youth's face became too mean. Two or three times during the
afternoon, as Cai climbed down the mountain, he thought about
the smiling face.

One morning, after his shower, Tudor placed my fingers to the right and just below his left nipple. His muscles were hard anyway, after all the workouts, and I couldn't feel the lump he said he'd found.

Over dinner that evening, Max got carried away describing the palace gardens on Isola Bella and Glain sat and watched him, all dewy-eyed. When they carried their coffees out onto the terrace, Cai remained at the table, aware of the stiffness in his calves and thighs after the daylong hike. Stretching his legs gently, he watched Marco, the waiter who'd served them, and tried not to think about his aching muscles. Marco had that slight stoop of so many tall men; an apology for having his head stuck above the crowd or just a habit developed from too many bumps against beams and door lintels? His skin was dark against the whiteness of his shirt. Perhaps there were sculptured curves concealed within the crisp cotton – muscles toned at a gym or worked out in the early morning along the lengths of a pool – but he looked too lean for his own good. His hair was slicked and spiky, as seemed to be the season's fashion, and blacker than shoe polish. When he lifted his head he always wore a smile that evoked a sense of well-being... and doubtless elicited generous tips. Cai sensed the rousing in his body. It surprised and shocked him: such feelings had been quiet for so long. And he remembered how the memory of the youth who'd served him bread and cheese had come back to him. Lingering over his *espresso*, he wrestled with the sense that he was betraying Tudor... and held on to the vain hope that Marco's cheerful eyes would hold him in a cruisy gaze.

After seeing two specialists, there was an operation to remove his breast, some of the lymph nodes under his arm and part of the chest wall muscles. He never showed me the scar... never let me draw my fingers gently over it, or run my tongue along its length. He never let me kiss it better.

Straw-coloured curls, some darker and tighter – still wet from the shower – softened the angular lines of his youthful face. His pale lips, moist from the grapefruit juice, were pursed at the glass's rim, his thoughts momentarily distracted. Behind his hazel eyes, dreams were still being dreamed as everyone about him, except Cai, broke their fast with salami and cheese, strong black coffee and chocolate croissants. The sun broke from the clouds and drenched him in brightness. Perplexed by the surges in his body, Cai stared at the man: he looked like one of the angels in a painting Max had liked so much that he'd brought the Isola Bella brochure down to dinner the previous evening to show Cai what he'd missed. A little girl in a high chair, her face blotched with Nutella, began to cry. The curly haired man lifted her onto his lap, muttered something in what Cai thought might be Dutch and kissed her cheek with those moist lips. It was a kiss Cai longed to taste. Glain, too distracted by her infatuation with Max, failed to sense Cai's reawakening.

Then there were long months of chemotherapy... with puking, hair loss and despair. Some of the outer circle, in whom we'd chosen not to confide, assumed it was AIDS related. It was funny how their assumption sat so easily with Tudor and me. Men didn't get breast cancer.

From Laveno, Cai planned to take the open bucket cable lift to Sasso Fermo and hike for a few hours on the ridge, seven hundred metres above the lake. Next to him in the queue for the early morning ferry stood a man about his own age. Cai noticed his sunken cheeks, weighed down by slate-grey bags beneath eyes of smudged brown... and the bluish, keloid scar that cut across his chin for more than an inch. The man said something in Italian to the middle-aged woman in the ticket booth that must have been funny because she laughed loudly. A group of impatient students, English Tory-types, pushed into the queue besides Cai, distracting him and drawing the opprobrium of the middle-aged Germans further back on the line. The man with the bluish scar moved down the long jetty and was lost in the crowd.

Cai saw him again, standing at the rail of the boat looking back at Cannero; he swept back the strands of hair that had blown across his face with nervous flicks of his fingers. Now he looked less sombre, the suggestion of a smile on his face. Cai watched him with no conscious motive. After some time the man turned towards Cai, and as if he'd sensed Cai's interest, he nodded, said 'Ciao,' and headed for the door that led into the bar.

About a year after we thought that everything was okay, the back pain started and the doctor said that perhaps he should have a scan.

He was standing with his elbow on the high counter, cigarette in hand, drinking an *espresso*. When he wasn't drinking, he rubbed the fibrous blotch on his chin with the thumb of the hand that held his cigarette, the smoke swirling about his face. Cai asked the girl, who looked too young to be a regular employee and was perhaps still at school and doing a summer job, for a bottle of mineral water.

'So, you're English,' the man said to Cai, surprising him. 'Do you want one?'

Cai looked at the open packet of Camels that was thrust towards him and wished that he smoked so that he'd have a reason to linger.

169

'I don't... but thanks,' he said, sounding apologetic.

'I studied in Newcastle for a year; do you know it?'

'No, not well. I'm from north Wales... other side of the country.'

'Ah... I climbed a mountain in Wales once, but I don't remember its name... too many consonants.'

'Welsh is like that,' Cai quipped with a smile.

'My name is Danilo Magistrini... my friends call me Dani.'

And the scan showed a tumour on the spine, which the surgeon said was inoperable. Of course, none of them would say how long he'd got.

Caught in Cai's gaze, Dani finished his coffee and said, 'Mine is from an accident when I was fourteen.' A curl of smoke rose as he stroked the scar again. 'I came off my brother's motorbike.'

Cai didn't know what to say and in the moments of his hesitation he considered the palpable strangeness of the intimacy into which their scars had seduced them.

'I guess you haven't made friends with yours yet, then,' Dani ventured.

Cai wanted to say, 'Well, fuck you Dani Magistrini,' but he remained silent and wondered what sort of friend got you noticed in such a way that you were scorned.

'I'm sorry, I didn't mean to offend you,' Dani said, seeing something in Cai's face that Cai hadn't intended to give away.

'It's not offence I'm feeling,' Cai said, and searched for words... but found none.

The two men looked at each other long enough for discomfort. In the moment before he turned to leave the bar, Cai wanted Dani to hold him.

Tudor didn't want to add months to life; he just wanted quality for the life that he had left. He wasn't religious, but he had this notion that all the advances of medicine had a lot to answer for: he wasn't going to allow his life, his spirit, to be held hostage in a rotting body that was past its use-by date. He thought that was a kind of idolatry. But he took all the pain relief they could offer him.

For a while, before climbing the steps that led to the ridge path, Cai watched the paragliders jump from Sasso Fermo's sheer cliff edge, into the void where the currents carried them out over the valley. The view across the lake aroused him... or perhaps it was Dani's kiss... and he felt more alive than he had in months.

At bedtime on the night that Tudor died, he kissed my scarred face to 'make it better' one last time.

High up on the ridge, Cai paused to catch his breath, drink some water and marvel at the view.

171

Fridolin's Dance

Having no children of his own, Elgan took great pleasure from being a godfather. Just being asked had always surprised him. Each time, he'd quizzed the parents about their motives... and their expectations. He knew himself well enough not to promise to remember birthdays, and he certainly wasn't going to do the religious and moral teaching! None of his university friends would palm off that responsibility onto him, despite the fact that he'd trained for the priesthood. Usually they'd respond to his probing by saying that they thought he'd be a good role model, to which he'd pretend to be sniffy and make some quip about being a gay seminarian, a gay priest or a de-frocked gay priest – depending on the period within that decade when all six of his godchildren, three boys and three girls, had been born.

Fridolin, the youngest, was 'the German godchild', fondly referred to as *mein Patenkind*, the second son of Jochen, Elgan's seminary roommate. Jochen had settled with his family in Potsdam after the Wall came down; they'd made their home in a crumbling lakeside villa purported to have been leased for a while to Marlene Dietrich when she made The Blue Angel at the nearby Babelsberg film studios. From their terrace the Glienicke Bridge looked grey and austere. Sometimes, when Elgan visited, he'd sit on that terrace and wonder about the spy swaps the bridge had witnessed during the Cold War.

Fridolin had been born some years after Elgan's shocking, but predictable, fall from grace. Thus freed from his priestly duties and Advent responsibilities, Elgan visited in the weeks before Christmas. The boy was just a toddler when they made *Weihnachtsplätzchen* together that first time, spilling flour and vanilla sugar, ground spices, chopped almonds and coloured sugar pearls around Heike's kitchen. With biscuit dough under their fingernails and in their hair they'd sung Christmas carols in German, and Fridolin's brother and sister had laughed at Elgan's pronunciation. Making Christmas cookies together became their little ritual. By the end of the third pre-Christmas visit, Fridolin could sing *Stille Nacht* in Welsh and English, and Elgan could tease him about his pronunciation. Then for a few years the weekend highlight was a visit to the Christmas market in Spandau. The year Fridolin was eight, a heavy winter storm restricted their movements and they trudged around Sanssouci Park through the knee-high snow, Fridolin sitting astride his *Patenonkel*'s shoulders. Another time, Fridolin's sister had decided that everyone should go along to the *Staatsballett* in Berlin to see The Nutcracker... the magic of dance cast its spell and the boy was enchanted.

When he enrolled at the Trinity Laban Conservatoire of Music and Dance in the weeks after the Olympic Games left town, Fridolin had hoped that Elgan would visit him in London. But their diaries had been difficult to synchronize and it was April before they could agree a rendezvous. The pre-Christmas bake-offs had long since been abandoned, but Fridolin had been at Elgan and Joseff's Civil Partnership in 2006, Elgan had attended Fridolin's first communion in 2008, and Fridolin and his father had visited Elgan and Jos at their remote hillside cottage deep in the folds of the Rhinog mountains in north Wales for a few days in the summer of 2009; after that visit their communication had become more regular, thanks to social media.

'But you're taller than I'd imagined,' Elgan said after they'd released one another from a long hug. He wondered whether he'd missed some of the more recent photos Fridolin had posted on his homepage.

'And your hair is more grey than I remember,' Fridolin said, with a broad, cheeky smile.

'I can't believe so many people have turned out for Margaret Thatcher's funeral,' Elgan said as they jostled amongst the crowds. 'Perhaps I should have messaged you. Trafalgar Square is probably not the place to be this morning.'

'She must have been someone important,' Fridolin said. 'Is she something to do with the Queen?'

'I suppose you didn't do much modern British history at that Berlin *Gymnasium*,' Elgan teased. 'Margaret Thatcher was the first woman Prime Minister here in Britain, in 1979.'

'That was fifteen years before I was born,' Fridolin said with a shrug, and a sweet smile intended to exonerate him from Elgan's accusation. 'And she's having all this,' he added with a sweep of his arm from the Strand to Whitehall, just as the funeral cortege came into sight. 'I don't think Angela Merkel, our first woman Chancellor, will be honoured in this way.'

'You'll have to do an internet search on her when you get home... maybe you'll get some sense of why she's getting a ceremonial funeral with full military honours.'

They watched the procession turn into Trafalgar Square to muted applause, broken by a lone voice only yards from them shouting 'Maggie, Maggie, burn in hell'. This anguished cry signalled a small group of onlookers to turn their backs as the hearse bearing her coffin passed by.

'Why do people hate her so much?' Fridolin asked.

'There's a nice café in the National Gallery,' Elgan said, taking Fridolin by the arm and pointing to a building on the other side of the square. 'Let's move away in case it gets nasty here.'

They drank coffee and Fridolin ate two scones with strawberry jam and clotted cream. Being a man-of-a-certain-age, Elgan soon needed the toilet and excused himself. On his return, Fridolin was fingering his iPhone.

'She was Prime Minister for a long time,' he said, closing down the internet link and pocketing his phone. 'And now I understand why one of the boys at Laban has been singing 'Ding, dong! The witch is dead' all week: he's from the south Wales valleys and I overheard him say something about how his father and grandfather used to be coal miners.'

'The miner's strike lasted a year in '84 to '85 and destroyed many communities across the country. Family members fell out over it, and whole villages took opposing sides; some of those bad relationships were never repaired. Many people believe she killed the coal industry in Britain and left tens of thousands of people without a livelihood.'

'But she won the war against Argentina, over those islands.'

'She did, indeed... but for many people in Wales that was a terrible time.'

'Were lots of Welsh soldiers killed?'

'I'm sure people from Wales were injured and killed in the fighting,' Elgan said, wondering how to simplify a complicated story. 'But... in the nineteenth century a Welsh colony was established in Patagonia –.'

'Really?' Fridolin interrupted. 'Why would people from Wales move to Argentina?'

'For the same reasons lots of Germans went to North America in the nineteenth century; social and political, economic and religious... and the Welsh especially wanted to try to preserve their language; the English were doing their best to stamp it out at that time.'

'So people in Wales saw Thatcher's war against Argentina as being a war against some of their own descendants, is that what you're saying?'

Elgan shrugged, and offered an open-handed gesture. 'I'm sure many in Wales waved the Union Flag when the British troops left for the Falkland Islands, but even today there are strong family ties between Wales and Patagonia.'

Fridolin pondered these things for some time and then, after a deep breath and a long sigh he said, 'I know you were a priest... but... do you hate her?'

Elgan ran his fingers through his cropped hair. "Do not be deceived,' Frido: 'God is not mocked, for whatever one sows, that will he also reap."

'So that's the priest's answer... you quote Scripture,' he said, and shrugged his shoulders implying both dissatisfaction and non-comprehension.

'Okay Frido... I'll try and do better,' Elgan offered, scratching his beard with both hands. 'Let me tell you two stories: Story number one – Margaret Thatcher did her first degree in Chemistry and worked for a while as a research chemist. As a scientist, she would have understood the need to back up her research findings with evidence, and if evidence could be produced to show that a process or procedure worked, other people might use that procedure without doing all the groundwork over again to prove it works. Are you following me?'

Fridolin nodded, 'I studied physics and chemistry until last year.'

'So, medicine and dentistry and even education took this concept and developed what's called evidence-based practice;

what you do in your teaching or your nursing practice is based on evidence... based on what works.'

'That's totally straightforward... so what?'

Elgan scratched his beard again. 'Did your dad ever tell you about how I was kicked out of the church and had to go and find another job?'

'I know you stopped being a priest but I don't know why that happened.'

'I fell in love with Jos and the church didn't like that, so... because I'd studied immunology and cell biology before training to be a priest I was able to get a job in the Public Health Department in Liverpool. This was just at the time when Britain had started to wake up to HIV and AIDS... and because Thatcher had all that scientific training she understood the huge public health challenge to prevent the spread of HIV. Although it must have gone against all of her Conservative instincts, she listened carefully to public health doctors and drug addiction service workers all over the country and agreed that the National Health Service should fund a prevention programme. That meant opening clinics for street drug users to be prescribed with methadone, syringe and needle exchange schemes so that injectors didn't have to share needles, the provision of free condoms to sex workers and gay men. Teams of outreach workers were employed to do public education with hard-to-reach groups of people deemed to be at risk of infection because of their behaviours. Margaret Thatcher saw to it that hundreds of millions of pounds of additional funding went to the health service to do this work, and I was lucky enough to be in the right place, at the right time, and I became one of the people managing that whole project in Liverpool.'

'I didn't know that you'd done that sort of work. Were you successful?'

'British cities have some of the lowest HIV infection rates anywhere in the world, and a lot of gay men came to understand the need for safer sex... but we still – nearly thirty years on – have a lot of people addicted to prescribed methadone. Perhaps it's the lesser of two evils.'

'Maybe,' Fridolin said thoughtfully.

'So... how can I hate the woman? Because of her public health policy I got five or six of the most challenging and fulfilling years of my professional working life; I got paid really well and was able to buy an apartment... and after being kicked out of the church I found a new purpose and a new direction.'

'She did some good then... not such a wicked witch –.'

'Ah... but wait,' Elgan said, waving a pointed finger. 'Story number two – Once upon a time there was a little book called *Jenny lives with Eric and Martin*, a children's picture book from Denmark. Five-year-old Jenny lives happily with her father, Eric, and his boyfriend Martin –.'

Fridolin laughed. 'And this is a story about Margaret Thatcher?' he quizzed.

Elgan nodded and continued, '–and in the book the three of them go to the laundrette together, and Jenny helps Martin prepare a surprise birthday party for Eric... just everyday scenes of ordinary family life. But Mrs Thatcher didn't like *that kind* of family; she actually referred to it as a *pretended family relationship*. She was horrified and disgusted that this children's picture book was being used in primary schools across London in the early 1980s to help children learn about different kinds of families, and help the children who came from such families to understand that there were others like them.' Elgan paused and wondered just how much background he needed to cover. 'You could search this story too, Fridolin. I'm giving you the very short version. Thatcher's government drew up legislation to stop Local

Education Authorities using this kind of teaching material, on the basis that it promoted homosexuality and presented homosexuality as a positive lifestyle.'

'But isn't that why my mum and dad asked you to be my *Patenonkel*... so that we would see how people can be different... and that it's okay?'

'I remember your mother telling me that her parents weren't so happy that I'd been chosen. They thought that an openly gay man as a godfather would be a bad influence.'

'Yes, but they're old –.'

'They're the same generation as Maggie, Frido.'

Fridolin reached across the table and took Elgan's hand. 'I love it that you're my *Patenonkel*,' he said. 'When I first thought that I might be gay it just wasn't a problem for me to talk with my dad and my mum, because of you.'

'Hmm, so maybe your grandparents were right,' Elgan offered – a joking provocation.

'Don't make fun about it. It's too important to me to make a joke like that.'

'I'm sorry.'

The silence that slipped between them was swept away when Fridolin rose from the table. 'Shall we walk for while?' he asked. 'I don't get to come into the central London very often.'

'Is there something specific you want to see?'

'No, let's just walk.'

The long, cold winter in Britain had postponed the spring. The trees in London's parks were still skeletal, the spring bulbs in floral borders just green shoots. But on that April afternoon of Baroness Thatcher's funeral the sun shone and tattooed young men lay bare-chested on the winter-weary grass.

'One of the final year students is choreographing a piece for his honours project and he's asked me to dance for him,' Fridolin ventured as they walked beside the Serpentine.

'Congratulations... that is exciting.'

'Yes... I'm the only first year student he's asked... but he wants me to dance without clothes... and I'm not sure I'm comfortable.'

'There's a lot of nudity in Contemporary Dance these days. It's something you'll have to decide, sometime.'

'I know. I like to see it; on the stage... it can be very beautiful.'

'Does being naked add anything to the piece he wants you to dance, or is he just being outrageous?'

'I think, from the way he described it, it has to be without clothes... and I'd love to do it. I just need to get more comfortable with being naked, but I don't know how.'

'In your rooms, at home, do you walk around without clothes?'

'It's been too cold, this winter!'

They both laughed.

'Do you like to swim? Maybe you could join a naturist swimming club.'

'I wouldn't know where to look... for a naturist swimming club I mean, I've got no problems seeing other people without clothes.'

'Are you... shy?' Elgan quizzed, wagging his little finger.

Fridolin looked blank for a moment. Elgan dropped his hand to his crotch, still wagging his little finger.

'Oh...' Fridolin giggled. 'I'm... average, I think. Maybe even bigger than average... I don't know... I haven't had much experience.' He bit his lip. 'Yes, I am shy, I think, and... what if I get hard, that would be so embarrassing.'

'I think you'd probably be concentrating so much on the dance, there'd be little chance of that happening.'

Fridolin's face twisted and he sighed. 'If I say no he'll look for someone else and think I'm... Ach, I don't know the English word for *prüde*.'

'Prudish... I guess. But you can only agree to do it if it feels right. Have you talked to any of the other students? Maybe some of them have already done it and–.'

'I talked to a couple of my girlfriends, but they're not sure they're ready either.'

'And what about talking to your teachers about it, they may have all sorts of ideas about how you decide to take that step.'

'I guess I don't want to be the one to ask because that draws attention to me.'

'You know, Frido, perhaps most of the first year students feel exactly the same way and are just desperate for someone to ask the question.'

'Well... maybe you're right.'

'Maybe, if you talk to the choreographer, he'd understand. Surely you'd have some weeks of rehearsal... and that would be enough time to either get comfortable... or get out.'

'That might be a solution,' Fridolin said, and kissed Elgan on the cheek.

On Old Compton Street, the gayest street in Soho, they ate an over-priced salad in an over-crowded restaurant staffed by over-exercised, intimidatingly beautiful young men. At the next table, three ancient and raucous queens who'd just returned from turning their backs on the Baroness, were discussing Margaret Thatcher's legacy, their camp affectation causing both amusement and consternation amongst the other diners. Fridolin picked up on 'pretended family relationships' and 'that fucking Section 28'.

'What they're talking about,' Fridolin whispered, nodding towards the queens. 'Is it to do with the kids' picture book you told me about this morning?'

'I never did finish that story, did I?' Elgan said, nodding his head in agreement. 'Section 28 of the Local Government Act 1988 was introduced to prohibit the promotion of homosexuality in schools.'

'But what does *promoting* homosexuality mean?'

'That was never really clarified, but the legislation caused confusion and fear in education circles and as a consequence, a majority within the teaching profession believed that teaching about homosexuality in the classroom was illegal.'

'How can learning about something important, that affects lots of people, be made illegal?'

'Just think about your grandparents for a minute... they probably still think I shouldn't have been your godfather.'

Fridolin pulled an anguished face and shrugged.

'Section 28 effected schools in a profound way for more than fifteen years,' Elgan ventured again. 'Efforts to recognise and systematically address homophobic bullying faltered because school governors and school managers were afraid of the possible consequences and there was virtually no support for students who chose to come out at school.'

'And still you don't hate her?' Fridolin said, but now it was almost an accusation.

"Hate is a lack of imagination," Elgan said.

'Ah... you're being a priest again... another quote!' Fridolin spat with frustration.

'Frido... don't be like this,' Elgan said, reaching for his hand. 'It's something one of Graham Greene's characters said in a novel, and I think it's true. Hate isn't so difficult... or creative. Some of us tried to respond to Thatcher's nastiness by using our imagination.'

Fridolin shook his head dismissively: 'And?'

'We organised, Frido. It didn't happen overnight... it took years, but we organised.'

'And?' he said again.

'Slowly, the lesbian and gay community in Britain found a voice – a strong political voice. Thatcher was only successful with Section 28 because there was no organised, articulate opposition from the gay community... that only developed as a reaction to her legislation. A really strong lobbying group called Stonewall was founded, with supporters from all over Britain; lawyers and doctors; teachers and civil servants; people in the military; actors, movie stars and writers... and plumbers and electricians and secretaries. Stonewall attracted people from all walks of life, and through the 1990s it learned how to lobby individual politicians, parliament and people in the public eye.'

'And?' he said again, but this time with anticipation.

'And really slowly... it took years... hearts and minds were changed: in 2002 gays and lesbians won the right to adopt children; anti-gay hate crimes were recognised in law by 2003, the Civil Partnership Act came in 2004, so Jos and I were able to get married – well, *civilised* anyway, there's legislation to prevent us being discriminated against in the workplace, we have equal access to goods and services – so no hotel in Britain can refuse Jos and me a double bed. Perhaps none of this would have happened if there had been no Margaret Thatcher.'

'May she rot in hell,' the three queens at the next table said in unison as their champagne glasses clinked.

Elgan rotated the band of Welsh gold Jos had given him to celebrate the legal recognition that they'd claimed in April 2006 – after more than twenty years together. 'We decided to stick with love because hate is too great a burden to bear.'

Fridolin smiled. 'My grandparents are so wrong about you,' he said.

They smiled at one another across their table.

'So, my lovely Frido,' Elgan said. 'When do I get to come and see you dance?'

Kiss and Tell

Some of the girls in Seimon's class already seemed much older – and a bit scary. Often they'd huddle into exclusive, whispering broods, and there'd be audible sighs and sometimes shrieks of laughter above their murmuring, and furtive glances at no-one-in-particular. A couple acted like they'd already outgrown their peers; Jane Jones, who'd got breasts that were the Promised Land of boys' dirty talk, almost always had love bites on her neck, and Shân Jenkins boasted about going to the nightclub in Llandudno at the weekends with her boyfriend, who was a management trainee with one of the new, cheap German supermarkets. There was even a rumour that Shân was on the pill.

Seimon had decided it wasn't easy being fourteen. Most of his classmates had started to muscle-up, which made rugby more of a man's game; it made the showers afterwards a real embarrassment too. Naked and puny amongst so many well-developed boy-men, he just wanted to disappear. He knew that puberty kicked-in later in some, but why did he have to be the runt, and bear the brunt of so much teasing? Sometimes he imagined himself smaller-than-small so that the others wouldn't notice him – and sometimes they didn't. But then, when the boys he hung around with seemed not to want to see him, he wondered if he'd made himself too insignificant. Being lonely was horrible. Feeling isolated, he doubted himself even more.

At first he'd just daydreamed about Mr Roberts; in Seimon's

mind's eye, his favourite teacher would be reading to the class – one of the poems they were studying in a literature project, or perhaps he'd be explaining something about the vagaries of Welsh grammar. Seimon found him fascinating to watch; those hands, with long delicate fingers, always expressive, and that face so animated with passion for his subject and the love of teaching. Then, in one of his early reveries, his teacher smiled at him. It was as if Seimon was the only other person in the classroom and Mr Roberts was only interested in him. The smile encouraged Seimon. Even Mr Roberts' eyes smiled, beckoning, inviting engagement with the poem, the grammatical foible, the infatuation... with language. And Seimon felt special.

Dylan Roberts had gone back into the closet against his better judgement. He could remember the day he'd made that decision; it was late spring and he was driving to the interview for the job as Head of Languages at the new secondary school on the coast. After a sharp burst of rain, from an errant cloud that hung in an otherwise blue sky, a rainbow arched over the growing forest of wind turbines out in Liverpool Bay. Only then did Dylan remember that he'd slapped a rainbow sticker onto the back window of his car after the Cardiff Gay Pride parade. He pulled over before reaching the school to peel it off; he couldn't see himself being out-and-proud in North Wales like he'd been in the capital. He'd got the job, on the strength that he could offer some German and French, and after selling his flat in one of the seedier Cardiff suburbs he'd bought a small house in Rhos-on-Sea, two streets parallel to the promenade.

In a small country, especially one that has recently gained some autonomy from its ruling neighbour, things can change quickly. By 2001 the Welsh Assembly Government was keen to hear from gays and lesbians across Wales – about their experiences of prejudice, their grievances and their aspirations. The new Minister for Education even made a thing about homophobic bullying in schools and in 2005 teachers were offered in-service training on how they could support gay and lesbian students in educational settings. Then Elton John married David Furnish and even the main Welsh language evening news on S4C carried the story.

Elton John was a favourite amongst many of the staff at Dylan's school. The television news coverage and the wedding photos in the newspapers invited unanticipated conversations in the staffroom: Tony Morris, the Head of Maths and three years off retirement, came out as the father of – not one, but two gay sons; Ann Puw, one of the history teachers, talked about her lesbian sister; Jane Edwards, the only newly-qualified teacher at school and not yet twenty-five, shared that she'd grown up in a lesbian household with two mums.

Over the Christmas holidays, Dylan considered these revelations and made a new year's resolution to come out at school. Most of the young women teachers had already guessed, since their attempts to flirt with Dylan had been rebuffed. Only one of his older male colleagues seemed less friendly. The head teacher, a dynamic forty-something in her first headship, praised Dylan for his courage and said he'd be a good role model for the four boys in years ten and eleven who'd come out.

Mr Roberts' coming out was *the* topic of conversation for a couple of weeks after the Christmas break. Jane Jones thought it was such a waste that someone as handsome and sexy as her Welsh teacher could be gay, and Shân Jenkins, who'd been ditched by the *Aldi* management trainee at a drunken New Year's Eve party, thought she might try to seduce him. A clutch of the rugby boys cackled a bit, but that was mostly to disguise their own insecurity. In fact, most of Dylan Roberts' students thought it was 'dead cool' that he was gay.

Seimon, though, was surprised... at first, anyway. He knew about gays and lesbians, of course; his parents had even been to a Civil Partnership – one of the very first gay weddings – a college friend of his dad's: Miriam. She was nice, but her partner Kate was built like a wrestler, and a bit like a man – with hairy arms and legs, and always wearing jeans and check shirts. He didn't really know any gay men, except the boys who'd come out at school, but like Graham Norton and Julian Clary on the television, they seemed so girly. He was taken aback when Mr Roberts came out because his teacher was so *normal*.

Seimon had been slow to discover that touching and rubbing parts of his body – well, *that* part especially, could feel nice, though he hadn't done it often because he'd overheard some of the rugby boys say that wanking could cause a deformity and even blindness. In the days after hearing that Mr Roberts was gay he wondered if his teacher did it... and whether he did it with other men. Seimon became aroused by these possibilities. For about a week he tried not to think such thoughts, but one night, in the privacy of his room and feeling secure under the duvet, he petted and stroked himself and imagined Mr Roberts doing the same. In some unexplainable way, imagining Mr Roberts masturbating made the possibility of deformity and blindness less credible. After that he did it more often and before too long they were touching one another; even his classroom daydreams became sexual fantasies.

Jane Jones had a reputation for offering boys the chance to explore the Promised Land, if they could afford it; for a pound they could touch her breasts through her school sweatshirt and for two-fifty she allowed their sweaty hands to grope through her bra. Just once she'd let a boy that she liked touch her bare breasts, but that had cost him a fiver. Jane always had money to buy cigarettes and blackcurrant VKs from the off-licence on the Esplanade, where no one ever asked her age.

'I'd let you touch-me-up for free,' Jane said to Seimon one day because she felt sorry for him, but she said it loud enough for some of the rugby boys to hear; she wanted to make Griff Thomas jealous. 'Only through my clothes though,' she taunted Seimon with a suggestive wink.

Seimon's face turned scarlet. Griff Thomas pushed to the front of the scrum of boy-men and, flicking two fingers at Jane, he sneered; 'Simple sissy Seimon wouldn't know what to do with them. You should see the way he looks at us in the showers.'

'You gay, like Mr Roberts, Seimon?' Jane gibed, loud enough to draw mocking jeers from Griff and his mates. 'Maybe if I give you a feel under my top it'll help you make up your mind.' As she said this she raised her sweatshirt until the pink bead in her navel ring was showing.

Seimon didn't know what to say, or do. That Jane was being so common with him didn't seem to matter too much, but in front of the boys he felt he needed to respond – and at least deny that he looked at them in the showers. But he did look at them in the showers.

Shân Jenkins was one of the Year Nine representatives on the School Council. Her election had surprised a lot of the teachers and some of the students. She took her responsibility as a Year Rep very seriously, almost as if she wanted to spite those that doubted her, and every Thursday lunch-time she'd walk around the school chatting to other students from her year and solicit their views about life in school.

'You're on your own a lot these days Sei,' she said, finding Seimon sitting by himself at the far end of the field. 'Ever thought of going to the Lunch-time Club?'

'I don't need the lonely kids club when I've got my dreams to keep me company,' he said, because it was hard for him to admit, even to Shân, that he was a bullied loner.

'What sorts of dreams d'you have then?' Shân coaxed, just to be friendly to a lonely kid.

Seimon hesitated, but recalling the gossip about Shân he suddenly felt emboldened. 'I was just imagining being kissed and cuddled by –' But then he panicked. He couldn't say *boyfriend*, not even to her. 'My lover,' he mumbled. The word was so alien to him.

'Well, Seimon Gwyn, who's a dark horse?' Shân exclaimed. 'Tell Auntie Shân some more.'

'Nothing to tell,' Sei said, feeling his confidence drain.

'Oh... come on, Sei. Who is he?'

She said *he* so matter-of-factly... so naturally, that he felt encouraged to tell her.

'It's Dylan,' he said, savouring the sense of importance it gave him, despite the fact that even in his imaginings his teacher was always Mr Roberts.

'Dylan Williams... in Year Eleven?' Shân said with confused curiosity. 'He's not gay; he's going out with Anwen who plays the harp in assembly sometimes.'

'No... Dylan Roberts, Welsh, French and German,' Sei said, more boldly than he'd intended.

'You're kidding, Sei,' she said, remembering the workshop they'd had about sexual abuse on the School Councillor training day – and remembering her own fantasy fling with her teacher after her *Aldi* management trainee had dumped her. 'Tell me you're just having me on.'

Feeling too important now to back-track, Seimon embellished his love affair.

On Thursday afternoons, Year Nine had History with Mrs Puw, who was also the School Council link teacher. Shân had begun to like history. Ann Puw offered her classes opportunities to do project work and Shân, with two of her friends, was investigating women's fashion through the twentieth century – and specifically how women's clothes reflected women's roles in society. The three girls had reached the nineteen-seventies and though their research into women's lib had been fascinating, Shân couldn't concentrate. She kept looking across the classroom to where Seimon was sitting, and found herself torn between feeling jealous that Sei had got-off with Mr Roberts and her responsibility as a School Councillor to report the sexual abuse to Mrs Puw. She kept remembering that the man who'd come to the School Council from the Children's Commissioner's office had emphasised that all children and young people had rights, but with rights there were responsibilities. At the end of the lesson she told Mrs Puw about Seimon and Mr Roberts and felt proud that she'd lived up to her responsibility.

Eleri Clwyd, the head teacher, spoke with a clarity and calmness that belied the nauseating clench of her stomach. Dylan was suddenly choking on the room's stuffiness and the abhorrence of the allegation against him. His union representative, a woman in her fifties with too much make-up and dark-rooted platinum hair that made her look tarty, reached across to touch his shoulder. She offered a faint smile of reassurance.

'You'll be suspended without prejudice pending further investigations,' Eleri Clwyd said.

Dylan's complexion turned the colour of cheap household

candles and his mouth seemed to fill with dry, gritty sand. There were questions he wanted to ask, but his usual fluency with language and lucidity of thought were shunted into a siding... and in his mind's eye there was only Seimon Gwyn, smiling.

Medi's Wedding Dress

Bryn Williams sat in the sagging easy chair by the fire, a mug cupped in his swollen, bent fingers. He supped his tea between rasping gasps for breath. Deliberately avoiding the table, where the only offering from the postman lay discarded with the remains of his breakfast, he took in the poky, nicotine-brown living room with its gallery of photographs; his life in dusty picture frames. Anwen, who'd put two logs on the embers before she'd made his toast and porridge, didn't take after her mother; if Bryn asked her to do a bit of cleaning she'd usually scoff and say something about her college education putting her above housework, and she'd whine about him not having a home-help. With the reviving warmth of the flames in the hearth he felt the old resentments rise.

'They used to send buggers to prison,' he snapped.

Washing-up the dishes her father had stacked on the draining board in the two days since her last visit, Anwen rinsed off her irritation with the soap suds. 'They used to send them to mental hospitals too,' she said matter-of-factly. She hadn't known this until she'd read the book Dylan had sent her. 'They used to give them electric shocks; some kind of aversion therapy.'

'During National Service they were dishonourably discharged... and now they can get married: it's a bloody sham. I don't know what that Tony Blair was thinking about.'

'It's called a Civil Partnership, Dada,' she said from the kitchen door, an indulgent grin on her face displacing her exasperation.

'Nothing civilised about sodomy,' he said into his tea.

'Oh, come on Dada,' she quipped, beginning to clear the table. She looked at the invitation her father had tossed aside earlier. 'Dylan's been with Eric for over twenty years, and now that the law has changed they want to celebrate—'

'Don't give me that rubbish, celebrate be damned,' Bryn said, his voice raised, croaky and broken. 'It's shameful... a damn disgrace on the whole family.'

'But he's your only boy, Dada. He's flesh and blood.'

'Better that we'd only had you girls then,' Bryn spat. 'I don't know what your mother would make of it all: turning in her grave she'll be.'

'Mama would have been on the first bus to Wrexham to buy a new hat, and you know it,' Anwen said, and turned back into the kitchen. 'She loved a party, and she loved us kids enough to want us to be happy, no matter what.' She heard him wheeze as he pulled himself up from the chair. 'And besides, Mama liked Eric.'

'Suppose you'll be going... to this charade then?' Bryn said, waving his empty mug and the invitation in his left hand, his right grasping the door frame to steady himself as he fought for breath. He still believed it was all the medication that was making him breathless; nothing to do with the forty-a-day over fifty or more years that had caused the emphysema.

'We're all going, Dada... of course,' she said with a sigh. 'The boys have asked Medi to be a bridesmaid.' As soon as she'd spoken she regretted her choice of words; she should have said flower girl or ring bearer, but somehow bridesmaid had just slipped off her tongue.

'Jesus Christ!' Bryn fought for air. 'Which one of them's the bride then, wearing the bloody dress?' His fingers, grasping the doorframe, turned white. 'I always thought that Eric was a bit like a female impersonator. And you're letting my only granddaughter be exposed to that? It's... perverted! My little *cariad* Medi shouldn't be–'

'She's only seven, Dada... and she's so excited.' Anwen pointed an accusing, sudsy finger at her father. 'Don't you spoil it for her. She loves her uncles, and I won't have you telling her it's wrong. Eric's a lovely lad and he makes Dylan happy; that's what's important. The world has moved on you know.'

'Moved on? It's gone off the rails.' He slid the empty mug onto the draining board and shuffled back to the chair by the fire, mumbling curses.

Eric stood in his Harrods-monogrammed dressing gown and turned the wooden spoon quickly in a pan of simmering water, à la one of those over-rated, over-paid TV chefs, before pouring the cracked egg gently from a cup into the vortex; his hips swayed gently, seductively, with the stirring. Because it was Saturday, Dylan fussed with the coffee; always *Illy*... three flat scoops... four cups of water... always drunk with hot milk and brown sugar – Muscovado, not Demerara. The *Today* programme on Radio 4 was churning out more bad news about the crunch of capitalism, but between the coffee and Eric's bum, Dylan wasn't listening.

'Perhaps we shouldn't have sent your dad an invitation,' Eric said, extracting a perfect poached egg from the pan with a slotted spoon. 'We already know that he won't come and the last thing we want to do is upset him.'

'But it's not for us to decide for him, Eric; he's got to make that decision for himself,' Dylan said, pouring their coffees.

'It's probably better that he doesn't come. He's not well; Anwen says it's made him really bad-tempered.'

'You're just being kind now. You know, as well as I do, that if he did come he'd be obnoxious; he'd like to see hanging brought back for the likes of us.'

'That's too extreme, Dylan. Bryn is just a bit of a dinosaur.'

'No – for all his union militancy, fighting for every worker's cause under the sun, he never got his head around sexuality as a rights issue... and if it hadn't been for Mam he'd have cut me off when I first came out.' Dylan pierced the yolk of his egg with a toast soldier.

Eric savoured his coffee and then dipped his croissant into it. 'Anwen will come with us when we take Medi to buy her dress for the wedding,' he said, half question, half assertion.

'She better had be coming with us,' Dylan said, a trickle of free-range-yellow yolk on his chin. 'I don't know the first thing about dresses for little girls.'

Anwen came through from the kitchen. 'I'll get you some fish when I go down the market,' she said. 'A nice piece of yellow haddock, yes? You can put it in the micro in a bowl of milk. It'll be lovely with some brown bread.'

Bryn ignored her. He threw the invitation into the grate and watched as the white card buckled and the gold calligraphy melted. Then the flames charred the affront of it all.

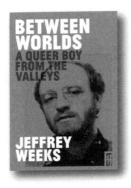

PARTHIAN Modern Wales

Between Worlds: A Queer Boy From The Valleys
JEFFREY WEEKS
ISBN 978-1-912681-88-4
£20.00 • Hardback

Just So You Know
ESSAYS OF EXPERIENCE
EDITED BY HANAN ISSA, DURRE
SHAHWAR AND ÖZGÜR UYANIK
ISBN 978-1-912681-82-2
£9.99 • Paperback

Rhys Davies: A Writer's Life
MEIC STEPHENS
ISBN 978-1-912109-96-8
£11.99 • Paperback

The Journey is Home

JOHN SAM JONES
ISBN 978-1-912681-74-7
£15 • HARDBACK

"People like John Sam Jones are the real unsung heroes of society. His work, and the work of his peers in public health and LGBTQ equality campaigning, mean that those growing up today face a different world from the one Jones was born into. It is easier to live without shame thanks to the work of those who went before. For this reason alone, it's important that Jones's story is heard. However, that is to say nothing of Jones's wonderful writing. His words are considered, his meaning is clear, and the complex issues and experiences he's faced are described with a roundness that is unexpected. Despite the traumatic nature of much of what's described, Jones's voice is without bitterness, resentment or anger, and it is clear that his own internal struggles and release of shame have resulted in him becoming who he is. His own journey is the making of him and it's a privilege that he chooses to share it."

Liam Nolan (A review from *www.gwales.com*, with the permission of the Books Council of Wales.)

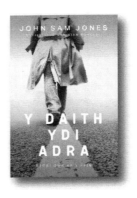

Y Daith Ydi Adra
(Cyf Sian Northey)

JOHN SAM JONES
ISBN 978-1-913640-45-3
£15 • Hardback

"Dyma gyfrol am ddyn sydd wedi torri ei gŵys ei hun ac sydd yn y pen draw wedi dod o hyd i'w *heimat*, ei 'adra'. Heddiw, dywed, mae yntau a Jupp yn mwynhau eu golygfa yn Effeld. "Yfory, neu ryw yfory arall – pwy a ŵyr?" Ie, y daith ydi adra, a diolch am gael ei rhannu."

Catrin Beard (Adolygiad oddi ar www.gwales.com, trwy ganiatâd Cyngor Llyfrau Cymru.)

PARTHIAN *Modern*

Martha, Jack & Shanco
CARYL LEWIS
TRANSLATED BY GWEN DAVIES
ISBN 978-1-912681-77-8
£9.99 • Paperback

Work Sex and Rugby
LEWIS DAVIES
ISBN 978-1-913640-23-1
£9.00 • Paperback

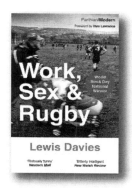

Fresh Apples
RACHEL TREZISE
ISBN 978-1-913640-26-2
£9.00 • Paperback

Queer Square Mile

Queer Short Stories from Wales

EDITED BY KIRSTI BOHATA, MIHANGEL MORGAN
AND HUW OSBORNE

ISBN 978-1-913640-24-8 • £20 • Hardback

The first anthology of its kind of Welsh fiction, with a
selection of over 40 short stories (1837-2018) including
work by Rhys Davies, John Sam Jones, Deborah Kay
Davies, David Llewellyn, Aled Islwyn, and Kate North.

the RHYS DAVIES TRUST